THE EVOLUTION OF

TWENTIETH-CENTURY HARM

# THE EVOLUTION OF

# TWENTIETH-CENTURY

# HARMONY

BY

WILFRID DUNWELL B.A., Mus.B. Ph.D.

LONDON

## NOVELLO AND CO. LTD.

160 WARDOUR ST. W.1.

First printed in 1960

*Copyright 1960 by Novello & Company Limited*

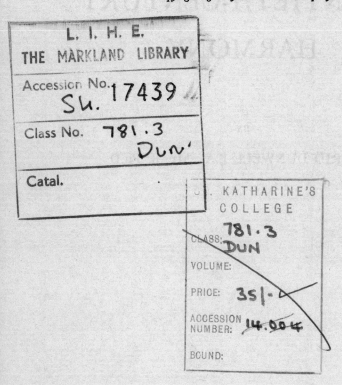
SET IN 11 ON 12 POINT BASKERVILLE
PRINTED AND BOUND IN GREAT BRITAIN
BY NOVELLO AND COMPANY LIMITED
LONDON W.I

# PREFACE

T<small>HIS</small> <small>BOOK</small> is based on material presented as a thesis
for the degree of Ph.D. (University of London)
in 1953.

My cordial thanks are given to Dr. William Lovelock for his unfailing patience in reading my drafts, for his keen and critical judgment, and for many friendly and helpful suggestions. To Mr. Norman Peterkin I am grateful for valuable advice in preparing these chapters for publication, and I also wish to thank the following publishers for permission to use musical quotations: Messrs Augener Ltd; Boosey and Hawkes Ltd; Chappell & Co., Ltd., London; J. & W. Chester Ltd; J. Curwen & Sons, Ltd; Durand et Cie; Jean Jobert; Oxford University Press; G. Schirmer, Inc., New York (Chappell & Co., Ltd., London); Schott & Co., Ltd; Stainer & Bell Ltd; Universal Editions A. G., Vienna (Alfred A. Kalmus, London); and Zenemukiado Vallalat of Budapest.

W<small>ILFRID</small> D<small>UNWELL</small>

# CONTENTS

# INTRODUCTION

THE USE of the word Harmony, in preference to the wider terms Music and Composition, sets limits to the scope of this study. It places emphasis on point-to-point details of technique and excludes the consideration of complete works and of personal styles. The purpose is not to add to the large body of critical and historical writing which already exists, but to try and answer the question 'Why does twentieth-century music sound so unlike earlier music?' Are composers using a completely new language, or the old one with a far wider vocabulary? If we look more closely at this language and increase our understanding of it, we may become more responsive to the musical thought it is conveying.

The objective is limited, and even so, not completely attainable, since creative thought often reaches beyond existing experience and in doing so makes new channels for its expression. The thought and its expression may often be inseparable. When Stravinsky opens the *Sacre du Printemps* with the bassoon placed high on the treble C, he is not only presenting the melody in a particular tone-colour. By pressing the instrument beyond its normal comfortable range he is producing a degree of tension which is an essential of the musical thought. In this sense, there are technical innovations which have no meaning in themselves apart from a particular musical experience. They may perhaps not recur, and hence do not fall into place in any regular technical system.

Not all creative thought requires an expanding language. New and significant experience may be communicated by giving fresh order to existing materials: Bach used no new harmonic or contrapuntal device in the 48, a work which was none the less a new creation in his own day, and remained new through the uniqueness of its musical thought. In the twentieth century, Hindemith's *Ludus Tonalis* recalls the method of that earlier work, in being a succession of preludes and fugues on every possible tonal centre. Like Bach, Hindemith has used no mode of expression that was not already in contemporary use, but he has added to the sum of creative musical thought. He has done so through a technical medium which has become more or less familiar.

It is possible then to find in contemporary music features which recur often enough to be recognized and analysed. If they cannot all be assessed apart from their musical contexts, it is still possible to illustrate the general development of twentieth-century technique.

Why has there been such a startling change in the character of music that it has become, for the general listener, a foreign and incomprehensible tongue? Languages are expected to preserve a recognizable continuity: changes occur, but not so suddenly as to obscure the parent stock. It is easy to record technical innovations and give a general answer to the question '*How* twentieth century music differs from earlier music?'; But it is not possible, by mere cataloguing, to answer the more searching question of '*Why* it differs'. The new technical details and the aesthetic motives behind them can only be appreciated if we abandon analogy, and use a precese definition. Music is the art of giving significant order to sounds: that is to say, the composer communicates with the listener by means of sounds set in relationships which have meaning.

Now the listener's mind is not a blank sheet; the incoming sounds, besides having their own order, induce reactions in the listener and so enter into a relationship with the mental and emotional states which exist actually or potentially within him as an individual. Music so heard can take on associations for the listener which may or may not have been in the mind of the composer. Sounds which for him had derived their meaning purely from their order may possibly be taken by the listener at that pure valuation, but they may equally well suggest something outside themselves, such as emotions, thoughts or pictorial images. Moreover, the composer himself has inherited a sum of musical impressions, shot through with associations, and he may either consciously or unconsciously contribute to this process of externalization.

This propensity for suggestion and association is very strong in music. Whether or not it is music's function to express something apart from the ordered relations of its own sounds will always remain arguable. As far as nineteenth-century romantic music is concerned far more was being read into the words 'significant order' than is warranted by a purely musical definition. The conception of music as a language had virtually superseded the conception of music as an art. It was not easy, in a period when Wagner had evolved his amazing musical and dramatic technique of expression, for a musician to eschew expressive urges and listen to the inner voice of his art. Nor was there in the Brahmsian stream, which flowed in channels worn by the classic forms, much real suggestion of the classical spirit; the emotional and intellectual states held sway also there. Is this perhaps a German racial characteristic? It is certainly not surprising that a reorientation which involved an inward turning of music upon itself should come from France, the home of subtle sensibility, precise thought, and elegant style. In Paris at the end of the nineteenth century the Symbolist poets were preoccupied above all with the purely musical quality of their verse, and the painters had turned from detail of external representation to the capturing of sense-impressions, and to the development of the medium of paint itself in solving problems of light. It was in the same way that Debussy, with an instinctive aversion from established convention in which sounds are links in a chain of thought, concerned himself with the quality of the sounds themselves, and so brought music back to its purer function of achieving significance in terms of its own medium.

What does this mean in technical terms? In Debussy's case it expressed itself in a new assessment of the materials of harmony, broadened to include new basic groups in addition to traditional triad structures. Debussy's clear discrimination between these various types will be illustrated (see page 75), after some technical examination has been made of their respective features. For the present, the noteworthy point is the fact that divergences of type have begun to exist at all. This is the sign of the working of the new leaven in music. It is remarkable that beneath all the varieties of personal style which abounded in the music before Debussy, there lay one common foundation, the triad system of harmony. Successive stages of elaboration, one leading to Bach, another to Beethoven, another to Wagner, differed in many respects; yet all had the same triad common denominator. What form could further developments take after Wagner? Would they involve still further complications of chromaticism and decoration on this well-tried basis? Debussy found another answer. He gave free rein to his own curiosity about the intrinsic interest of sounds, regardless of traditional authority; he was sensitive to new chordal shapes and colours; and he had the technical as well as the musical imagination to focus these shapes in a consistent system of harmony. His idiom preserved sufficient affinity with tradition to be lucid and coherent, but in it the monopoly of the triad was broken and its habits of progression were radically altered.

Implicit in this broadened basis, although not by any means fully apparent in Debussy's own work, is an unlimited expansion of discord. This showed itself first in acceptance of unprepared and unresolved dissonances, and then in an actual cult of discord as an inevitable part of the modern aesthetic view of music. Technical aspects of discord will loom large in this study and will be specifically discussed; but at all times the student of contemporary music must set any particular detail he may be analysing against the background of a high norm of dissonance. (For a closer definition of discord see p. 52 sqq. and p. 179.)

It might seem possible to study the new attitude to sounds from a purely twentieth-century angle, reviewing as a whole the results of technical explorations which have made the classical basis appear narrow. This approach, however, would give not only an incomplete picture, but a false one. In spite of the maze of new, and often strange, happenings in twentieth-century music, there has been no break in the continuity of fundamental development. There has been a quickening of change, but the foundations rest in tradition none the less. The approach proposed is therefore evolutionary, and the starting-point will be the classical system of harmony. Reference to the classical system, throughout this study, should be understood in a specifically technical sense. It will not be used to refer only to the style, forms, and musical thought of Haydn, Mozart, and Beethoven, but to describe the harmonic system which took shape in the seventeenth century, which continued as the foundation of the polyphony of Bach and Handel in the eighteenth century, and of the formalized style of the Viennese composers later in that century (normally referred to as the Classical composers), and persisted as the technical basis of the work of the Romantic composers of the nineteenth century. First, tendencies will be studied within that system which, pushed to extremes, could destroy its character.* These features will be studied under the general heading of Transition (conceived in a theoretical, not an historical sense), and they will be seen partly as logical developments of the old system, and partly as manifestations of the new urge to experiment in sound. The second part of the study will then be concerned with the various problems of organizing sounds on the considerably wider basis made available since the abandonment of the classical system.

A final definition should be added of the word *modern.* It is of course a relative term if used to refer to a period of time, but it carries a workaday meaning, and in some ways it expresses an attitude to art which is not necessarily implied by the terms *contemporary* or *twentieth-century.* There are inevitably overlappings, both in technical and aesthetic matters, between old and new. For instance, composers like Strauss and Elgar have worked during a third of the twentieth century at the same time as Bartok and Stravinsky, but the modes of thought

---

*There is a parallel here between the close of the nineteenth-century harmonic period and that of the sixteenth-century polyphonic one: in both cases, increased ranges of chromaticism and of emotional expression were exploited within the established system. It is obvious in the earlier case that this was a negation of the modal principles on which that polyphony was founded, and similar implications follow when attempts at expansion come into conflict with the conventions on which the classical harmonic system was based.

and technique of the first two men show no fundamental break with the main musical tradition, and offer no barriers to understanding by listeners who would on the other hand be nonplussed, not to say offended, by the works of the other pair of composers. 'Modernity' implies an attitude to art which is different in quality, not merely later in time, and which began to reveal itself, in relation to classical technique, at various points before the close of the nineteenth century. To trace its principles, origins, and varied manifestations is not within the scope of the present study; the aesthetic attitude which it presupposes is a composite thing, not to be defined outright or deduced merely from the technical by-products in any field. It is thus in the sense of an aesthetic attitude, not of a relative position in time, that the word will be used in this book.

# PART ONE

## *TRANSITION*

THE CLASSICAL SYSTEM of harmony is based on the major and minor scales, with their particular order of tones and semitones. From this choice, three characteristics follow, without which the system would lose its definition. The first concerns the method of chord-building; the second, the relation of these chords to one another and to their common tonal centre; and the third, the character of melody which is determined by that chord system.

The basic unit in chord-structure is the triad, which consists of two superimposed thirds, one major, one minor. Extension is made from this basis by the addition of further thirds, giving chords of the seventh, ninth, eleventh, and thirteenth; and by contrapuntal movement, which produces decoration and temporary discord, always logically resolved so as to relate it to the basic harmony. The use of chromaticism and modulation can be regarded as supplementary to the diatonic scale, just as decoration is supplementary to the chordal unit. The division of the diatonic scale into tones and semitones accounts for the alternation of major and minor thirds in chord-building, and for the varied interplay of intervals in the progression of parts. Certain features are avoided, or kept subordinate. Thus, chords are not built up of exactly equal intervals; like intervals do not follow one another in regular succession; separate parts do not maintain continuous parallel movement. The harmonic flavour depends essentially on the constant mixture and alternation of thirds, fifths, sixths, sevenths, and so on, in blend and contrast.

There is obviously room for flexibility of interpretation within such a system, and some features can be studied which in their first shape are only modifications of traditional practice, but in their final implications are quite incompatible with its conventions. The next chapter is concerned with two opposite approaches to the presentation of familiar chords in new lights. On the one hand there is the emergence of perfect fourths and fifths, with their starker quality, in preference to the sweeter thirds and sixths, which provided the common blend in the classical system. Chords can be arranged to bring these intervals into greater prominence, particularly when chords of the seventh and the various elements of the chord of the thirteenth are used more freely. The other method, at the opposite extreme to this rarefied atmosphere of harmony, is to present chords wrapped up in layers of added notes, as though to avoid any chance of their being recognized as triads. Different as they are, and apparently only superficial new fashions in the restatement of old truths, both these methods are symptoms of a new way of musical thinking, one in which more attention is paid to the intrinsic interest of sound-groups themselves than to their function as part of a musical language for the expression of ideas and emotions external to music.

This new attitude also underlies another type of modification of the classical triad which is examined in Chapter Two. A more fundamental characteristic of harmony is affected in this case, when the intervals of a triad are altered in such a way as to disturb the balance and contrast of its major and minor thirds. The augmented fifth chord, with its two superimposed major thirds, is in conflict with the basic principle of contrasted intervals selected from the diatonic scale-system, and it will be seen also that the other chords associated with the whole-tone scale play a large part in the disintegration of the traditional system of harmony.

The second of the defining characteristics, the relation of chords to a tonic through certain root progressions, arises from the fixed order of tones and semitones in the scale, and gives a particular cast to classical harmony by which it is distinguishable both from earlier and later music. The clear outlines of its system became increasingly blurred in the work of the nineteenth-century romantic composers, as more free and varied juxtapositions of chords were made familiar. The logical end of the process, which is outlined in Chapter Three, was reached in a system of harmony based not on the diatonic scales but on a scale of twelve equally available semitones. Supplementing this freer juxtaposition of chords was another strand of development, that of decoration applied to the underlying chordal basis. This process, which was one of constant absorption of discord and complexity into the harmonic texture, was common in the history of classical music; indeed, in the works of J. S. Bach it contributed a wealth of harmonic resource. It was greatly accelerated in the works of the romantic composers. The way in which this trend was exploited to achieve new sonorities and ultimately new views both of chord structure and of chord progression is the subject of Chapters Four and Five.

The controlling influence in such decorative movement, if it is to be anything more than merely superimposed ornament, is a contrapuntal one. This was more apparent at the beginning and at the end of the period which we have broadly defined as classical, in the contrapuntal harmony of Bach and Wagner. In the intervening highly formalized phase of development, the horizontal (melodic) aspect of music was closely controlled by the vertical (chordal) one; the latter could lend itself to separate study as an individual subject under the name of Harmony, and melodic features had perforce to be explicable as outlinings or decorations of its essential structural core. In Wagner's phrase, melody was the 'surface of harmony'. As long as tonal organization was planned on the basis of chord- and key-progression within the two limiting scales, melody, whether simple or complex, was bound to be a form of outlining or decoration of those basic chordal units. It could not be allowed to develop contours which would obscure any of the structural essentials of the key.

Here then is a third defining characteristic of classical music, one which results from the exclusion of certain melodic elements in order to preserve a particular convention of tonal organization. The balance of the whole synthesis is disturbed if the conception of melody is broadened to include all semitones on equal terms, or if it is based, like modal melody, on tones

B

and semitones in non-classical order. The influence of modes, the twelve-note* scale, and the whole-tone scale, had strongly asserted itself by the end of the nineteenth century; and in proportion as such influences prevail as consistent characteristics in a work, rather than as occasional features of a generally diatonic picture, so may the modern view be said to have superseded the classical. The detailed examination of such melodic organization will be made in the second part of this book. Meanwhile, the transition from classical to modern method will be seen to involve developments from harmonic starting-points which culminate in a new melodic conception as the foundation of twentieth-century composition.

In this review of the broad lines of transition, the years at the turn of the century have been mentioned more than once. It should perhaps be repeated that the present enquiry is not an historical one but rather an examination of method in the abstract, and that features discussed under the elastic heading of 'transition' cannot be pin-pointed in time or attributed exclusively to certain composers.

---

*The term 'twelve-note' will be used in this book to refer to the scale in which all semitones within the octave are equally available as the basis of harmony. 'Chromatic' will refer to the colouring of a diatonic scale, as in classical practice. Reference to the system evolved by Schönberg will only be intended when capital letters are used, thus: Twelve-Note System.

# CHAPTER ONE

# FOURTHS AND FIFTHS

A TRIAD lacks complete definition if its third is omitted, and the resultant interval, a perfect fifth in root position or a perfect fourth in inversion, has a bare effect which sounds assertive in the environment of classical harmony with its interplay of varied intervals. A comparatively fresh and simple resource is therefore available merely by giving to these two intervals a prominence which they were denied in traditional harmony. Exx. 1 and 2 emphasize their particular quality with scarcely any infringement of classical rules.

There is no new grammatical issue involved here, but there is a new flavour of harmony, obtained either by spacing of the chords (Exx. 1a and b), or by adjustment of decorative features (Exx. 1c and 2), to bring the fourths and fifths into prominence. The contrast between Ex. 2 and any typical

Ex.1 DEBUSSY No.3 from *Children's Corner*

Music extracts reprinted by permission of Durand & Cie.

Ex.2 IRELAND Rhapsody for Piano
(quasi cadenza)

Music extract reprinted by permission of Boosey & Hawkes Ltd.

Ex.3 FRANK BRIDGE *Water Nymphs*

Music extract reprinted by permission of Boosey & Hawkes Ltd.

cadenza of Chopin or Liszt is a measure of the shift of emphasis away from the classical blend of thirds and sixths.

Ex. 3, which is the final bar of one of Frank Bridge's piano pieces, not only shows the sharper edge which results from the deliberate isolation of the perfect fourths in the right hand, but illustrates one aspect of the modern attitude to discord in general. The dotted minim C sharp in the treble stave is the major seventh of the final chord, and it is allowed to fade quietly without resolution. The chord of the seventh so produced is not used in the classical way, as a temporary discord in a continuous web of part-writing; it exists in its own right and for its own colour, rather than for its tension in relation to an abstract basis. Developments in pianistic style, initiated by Chopin and Liszt, played an important part in the acclimatization of such experimental groupings, as also did isolated colour effects in opera from Glinka to Verdi. Concurrently with these new findings in separate sonorities, the general average of dissonance was being intensified in the further complication of traditional instrumental polyphony by Wagner and Strauss.

The two methods increasingly interact; it would not serve the purpose of the present study to seek the historical origins of modern innovations in one stream rather than the other, but for purposes of analysis the two can be separated, and it is particularly easy in the case of the perfect fourths and fifths to see the operation of one phase of reaction against classical structure in thirds. Ex. 3 shows the perfect fourth making its character felt as part of a composite group, and in the direction of sharper dissonance. The other examples point rather to the character of austerity and elemental simplicity which belong to the perfect fifth. Its influence as a corrective to over-luxuriant and complicated harmony has persisted in a vein of economy which has run side by side with more adventurous experiments.

It is scarcely possible to refer to the austere and elemental aspects of the fourths and fifths without recalling the ancient practice of Organum, though any idea of conscious revival of an earlier device seems hardly worth entertaining. (See also p. 85). It is more pertinent to note the varying position which the fourth has held in Western music. It began its career as a concord, in the period of Organum, and after thirds and sixths had become absorbed as concords, the fourth came to hold an indeterminate position, concordant between any two upper parts but discordant between any upper part and the bass. This was its academic status in classical harmony.

The focusing of attention on separate points of colour leads to new views of part-writing, which are illustrated in Ex. 4. In this example, the consecutive fifths in bar (fig.) 1 scarcely depart from traditional practice, as they result merely from redistribution of notes within the same chord. In the following bars however the principle of movement is new. Such use of parallelism is modern and not classical (see p. 87); but the origin of the device is suggested in bar one, which owes its character to the choice of the perfect fifth, and to a spacing of parts which brings that interval consistently to the fore.

The consecutive ninths in bar two produce a friction which was contrary to strict practice in classical part-writing but was rapidly assimilated as a normal concomitant of movement in the transitional phase. The whole attitude to the use of consecutive fifths, octaves, and discords, is necessarily transformed when the classical balance of dissonance and consonance is so completely disturbed by the two streams of development referred to on page 20.

The redistribution of parts of the same chord is carried a stage further in Ex. 5(a). The harmony on the root C lasts for four bars, and the traditional chord of the thirteenth would account for the notes B flat, D, and A, which occur in the upper parts. Free interchange then takes place among notes of the same chord, and there is no sense of separate chord-progression in the movement of the parts. If this extended view of movement over one chord is accepted, the bracketed phrase in Ex. 5(b) can be grammatically related to past practice, but it acquires a completely new emphasis and an unambiguously modern application when it is continued as an ostinato in the bars which follow this extract.

The general tendencies revealed in this passage are towards free use of the higher 'fundamental discords', (the seventh, ninth, eleventh, and thirteenth), but in such a way that the melodic shape and harmonic colour arise from the cultivation of a particular interval.

Increased interest in the sensuous effect of individual sound-groups also accounts for the procedure in Ex. 6. The purpose is the same as that underlying the new cult of fourths and fifths, to derive new colours from old materials; but the effect on the musical texture is very different. Instead of clarity of effect and economy of means, there is a preference for blurred outlines, and there is no sparing of notes. Analysed in technical terms, this final chord of G flat has the appoggiaturas A flat, E flat, and F, added to it and left unresolved. The added notes (carrying with them incidentally a strong suggestion of upper partials) have not their traditional function of forming links in a horizontal progression, though in fact in this example the mental effect of their resolution is easily felt. They are presented rather in a new aspect: their original purpose being taken for granted, they are absorbed into the main fabric for their contribution to harmonic colour. The dominant seventh began its independent existence as a chord in similar fashion, to be followed by the remaining sevenths and derivatives of the triad. In this process, the interval of the major second, which occurs between the seventh and the root, became an almost inevitable component of harmonic texture, especially noticeable when brought within the stretch of the hand in piano

Ex. 4 VAUGHAN WILLIAMS No. 3 of *Five Mystical Songs*

Music extract reprinted by permission of Stainer & Bell Ltd.

Ex. 5 FRANK BRIDGE Cello Sonata

Music extract reprinted by permission of Boosey & Hawkes Ltd.

Ex. 6 FRANK BRIDGE *Ecstasy*

Music extract reprinted by permission of Augener Ltd.

Ex.7 WARLOCK *Jillian of Berry*

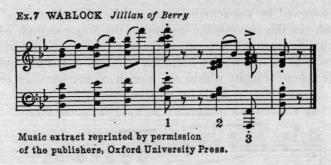

Music extract reprinted by permission
of the publishers, Oxford University Press.

music.  The step from regarding this interval as part of a
theoretical chord to using it as an element in any sound cluster
was not difficult, especially when new sonorities were being
deliberately cultivated.  One style of writing emerged in the
early twentieth century which depended more on superficial
exploitation of such external features than on a true sense of
harmonic colour.  On the other hand, though the method can
be a *reductio ad absurdum* if it merely consists of surface additions
to an already complete system of harmony, the principle of
seeking interesting sonorities for their own sake was fruitful.

Technical analysis will show that in a large number of cases
apparently added notes are really fundamental discords,
(ninths, elevenths, thirteenths), or decorations like passing-notes
and appoggiaturas used together with triad notes which in
traditional practice they normally displaced.  See the first four
chords of Ex. 7.  The spacing of the chords with fourths and
seconds in prominence contributes largely to their special
sonority.  Since the complete chord of the thirteenth
contains every note of the scale, any diatonic combination can
theoretically be explained on these lines.  The chords marked
1, 2, and 3, however, in Ex. 7, show a deliberate clustering of
these notes so as to produce a splash of piano tone rather than a
recognizable chord.  Reference to Ex. 42, which is quoted from
Bartok's *Mikrokosmos** should be made, to see the double

---

*This collection of Progressive Piano Pieces in six volumes, published by Boosey
& Hawkes, is invaluable for the clues it gives to the many-sided experimental
approaches that are possible in modern composition.

aspect from which these sound-clusters can be viewed. In that example they arise from part-movements which explain their origin, but in the last bars they are fully established as units in themselves.

# CHAPTER TWO

# THE AUGMENTED FIFTH TRIAD
# AND THE WHOLE-TONE SCALE

THE AUGMENTED FIFTH TRIAD in classical practice is produced by decoration of basic triads of the scale; any apparent occurrence in its own right, as in Ex. 8, is due to elliptical omission of a note of resolution. The chord does not form part of normal basic harmony; in fact, in relation to the diatonic system it has a mercurial quality and obstinately evades assimilation.

Numerous examples of its use for abnormal effect are to be found at various stages of musical history, as in Gibbons' *The Silver Swan*, Purcell's *King Arthur*, Liszt's *Faust Symphony*, and the *Ride of the Valkyries* of Wagner. In the *Faust Symphony*, in fact, the augmented fifth is used not only for its momentary dissolution of tonality, but as an integral part of the thought of the work, in portraying the Mephistophelian transformation in the Scherzo.

Ex. 8

If the augmented triad, with its two equal major thirds, so obstinately evades assimilation in the traditional harmonic system, a completely new view of harmony must be implied by the quotation in Ex. 9 from Debussy's *Fêtes Galantes*. The triad here has become part of the normal harmonic fabric, and does not require any expressive intention external to the music itself to account for its presence. To reach such a point,

Ex.9 DEBUSSY 'Le Faune' from *Fêtes Galantes*

Music extract reprinted by permission of Durand & Cie.

there has clearly been both a re-assessment of aesthetic values
and an enlargement of technical resources. In the matter of
technique, the transition was facilitated by the imaginative
innovations of Liszt and Wagner, both specifically with regard
to the augmented triad itself, and generally in the great
widening of chromatic scope, seen especially in *Tristan*. It was
further speeded by conscious experiment in whole-tone effects
among the Russian nationalist composers. (Significantly, the
whole-tone devices in their work are commonly associated with
supernatural characters in opera; Rimsky-Korsakov's *Snow-
Maiden* is an obvious example, and the principle was still at
work as late as 1909 in Stravinsky's *Fire-Bird*.) Considerable
space would be required to give a historical review of the
appearances of these chords in nineteenth-century music. The
general fact would still be confirmed that the augmented fifth
chord (and whole-tone harmonies in general), while becoming
more familiar as the century progressed, resisted full incorporation into the main stream of harmonic development until the
whole basis of harmony was broadened to include shapes other
than the triad and scales other than the major and minor.

Nineteenth-century expansion of resources for expressive
effect produced the technical raw materials. The strongest
factor in broadening the basis upon which these resources
could be assimilated was Debussy's cult of sounds for their
own sake. This sensuous attitude to harmonic phenomena
(already seen at work in the previous chapter) accounts for
the spate of harmonic innovations which flowed into music
at the turn of the century. The traditional idea of a balanced
interplay of parts and of varied intervals was superseded in

this phase of development. A fresh approach to the treatment of musical materials had begun, which no longer involved increasingly complex developments on old foundations, but was characterized by rapid assimilation of many new elements, and within a short time, new methods of organizing those elements. The most immediately striking among these extensions of the vocabulary were the harmonies associated with the whole-tone scale.

The whole-tone scale can be formed by using six successive tones from any starting-point in the two series shown at Ex. 10 (a) and (b). Enharmonic notation is freely employed in writing the scale and its chords.

In Ex. 11 are shown the various types of combination which can be derived from the first of these two series; semitone transposition would reproduce them in the second series. It is obvious at once that there are strong links with tradition as well as suggestions of new import; context alone can bring out the respective harmonic flavours. The two-note groups at Ex. 11a look backward, those at b look forward, in so far as they are treated as complete sound units in themselves, and not as part of chords of the seventh requiring resolution. Ex. 11c, from *Ce qu'a vu le vent d'Ouest* in Debussy's first book of Preludes, shows their modern application. Among the three-note groups (d), affinity with the past is clear, since all can be explained as either ninths, sevenths, or chromatically altered sevenths. At e there is the augmented fifth chord, and a group which may be either a traditional one (as seen in the enharmonic version in brackets), or a form of the chord shown below at Ex. 12b.

The form in which the whole-tone harmonies begin to exert their influence in a modern direction is seen in the four-part chords at Ex. 12 a, b, and c. The first four notes of the scale can occur in four different forms, if enharmonic changes

Ex.10

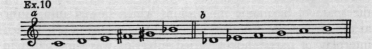

are used. The first, on the root D, is again a traditional ninth, but the remaining chords do not have a perfect fifth. They have either a sharpened fourth from the root, or a sharpened fifth, or both. Their simplest forms are shown at *b* and *c*. All other possible four-note groups will produce either this type

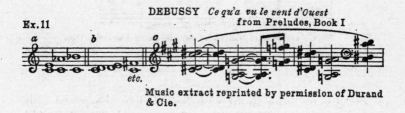

Music extract reprinted by permission of Durand & Cie.

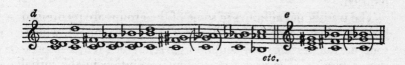

(Ex.13)

Music extracts reprinted by permission of Durand & Cie.

of seventh- or ninth-chord with flattened or sharpened fifth, or the augmented fifth chord, or the major ninth with its fifth omitted.

The traditional affinities of some of the groups are mentioned because they account for the easy incorporation of whole-tone harmonies into the common currency of French impressionist music. There was no violent revolution in the initial process. Debussy's String Quartet, which appeared in 1893, relies for its harmonic materials on triads, sevenths, and ninths used in a basically diatonic way, with chromatic features which are additional to, rather than an integral part of, the tonal structure. Yet in this environment occasional whole-tone harmonies can easily find a place. The influence on the character of melody as well as on harmony is to be noticed in the cello part of Ex. 13a, and the foreshadowing of a new fluidity in harmonic progression at b, which ushers in the recapitulation with a distinctly non-classical approach.

The quality of fluidity and indeterminacy, though negative in itself, was the most potent factor in completing the disintegration of the classical method of tonal organization. The fundamental assumptions in this method were not questioned until Debussy's innovations imparted a different quality to chords themselves. Chords no longer needed to be considered as links in a musical argument; there was no normal expectancy of progression, but rather a flux of colour, which could make its impression without the explanatory assistance of detailed drawing. The whole-tone chords, with their consistent level of mild dissonance, with no perfect fifths and fourths, deriving from a scale having no landmarks in the form of semitones by which progression could be directed to particular notes, were the most obviously lacking in all the requirements of classical tonality. They lacked also sufficient variety and generating power to provide in themselves an adequate alternative to that system. But during their vogue as fascinating novelties they made familiar a conception of harmony widened to include twelve semitones on an equal footing, and not conditioned by methods of progression which had grown up in association with diatonic scales and modes.

The return to the principal subject, in the first movement of the Ravel Quartet (1902), is effected by taking advantage of this kind of tonal ambiguity (Ex. 14). A few bars before this extract, the chord of the seventh on F sharp has been firmly established as the climax of the development section, but the play between its sharpened fourth and fifth (the C natural and D natural) permits the double-entendre in bar two, where the dominant seventh on root C emerges enharmonically. The cello restores the root F sharp in bar four, but the whole-tone ambiguity persists in the second violin, and the progression is maintained right up to the F natural chord of the recapitulation. A still more flexible treatment of chordal progression is to be seen in the last sixteen bars of the same movement based on the whole-tone steps shown in Ex. 15.

The simple means of these early stages were soon to suggest the possibility of far more complex textures. As far as the transitional stage is concerned, the whole-tone chords easily arise as chromatic alterations of traditional chords, governed by the customary root relations or by the contrapuntal movement of parts; they may be produced by decoration, or be themselves decorated. The chords of the seventh and ninth may be used without resolution, this being one of the expansions of dissonance which followed inevitably from the use of chords as separate points of colour. (Free resolution had already been used in isolated cases, e.g. the opening of *Tristan*, but it was not normal to use such chords as free units.)

**Ex. 14  RAVEL  String Quartet, first movement**

Music extract reprinted by permission of Durand & Cie.

**Ex. 15**

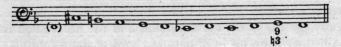

**Ex. 16  RAVEL  String Quartet, third movement**

Ex.17 IRELAND Rhapsody for Piano

Music extract reprinted by permission of Boosey & Hawkes Ltd.

Ex. 16 appears to convey a suggestion of bitonality. Ravel has written the chord enharmonically, except for its root E flat, for convenience of notation. It is a seventh with sharpened fourth and fifth, and with a minor ninth added, as seen at *b*. The F sharp in bars one and three is an auxiliary note, (equivalent to G flat), decorating the minor ninth (F flat) and resolved elliptically as indicated at *c*. There is no true bitonal effect to the ear, and the underlying whole-tone chord emerges unmistakably as one undivided harmony; but there is a sufficiently strong hint of the possibility of separate strands with their own tonal trends.

The disposition of the parts in Ex. 17 shows a similar play on the disruptive tendencies inherent in chromatic chords, though the arrangement of the same notes shown at *b*, or *c*, reveals only one basic chord. Bitonal suggestions will appear again as other harmonic innovations are examined, and it is not surprising that in a period of re-orientation and experiment their potentialities were developed far beyond the mere re-arrangement of notes within one chord.

# CHAPTER THREE

# NEW JUXTAPOSITIONS OF CHORDS

ONE FUNDAMENTAL CHARACTERISTIC of classical harmony, as has been seen, lost its definition as a result of modifications applied to the basic unit, the triad. Another principle is challenged, even if the triads are kept intact, when they are set in new relationships to one another in such a way as to disturb the traditional tonal organization. This depended largely on two physical properties of sound: the pronounced melodic leading effect of the semitone, and the strong affinity of any one chord with another whose root is a fifth lower. In diatonic scales, semitone steps are limited in number; and by their fixed position they bring their leading effect to bear always in the same place and focus attention on the primary triads, I, IV, V, as the defining elements of a key. Much chromaticism was easily assimilated into the classical scheme on this basis of root relations, or as superficial decoration; but it was essential to the coherence of the whole structure that the separate features, however complex or remotely connected, should be ultimately bound up in their root progressions with a central tonic.

The modern view prevails in proportion as these chromatic enrichments are not controlled by a basic diatonic scheme, but break its continuity or so enlarge it that other methods are needed to supplement the traditional one of root progression. Temporary interruptions of continuity were exploited in the classical sonata form itself, like the semitone shift of key from E flat to E which ushers in the coda of the Rondo in Beethoven's Op. 7 Sonata. Against a clearly established tonal background, such side-steppings can have an arresting effect which is not so easily attainable in a continuously chromatic environment. It is in this effect of unusual juxtaposition that

another significant modern development can be found.  If
these chordal movements are accepted as normal successions of
harmony, they blur the outlines of the classical method of
control by root-relationship, and by opening up free movement
among chromatic chords they lead outwards from the diatonic
to the twelve-note scale.  They can be studied in decorative
features applied to basic harmony and in the harmonic
structure itself.

### Decorative Juxtapositions

The decorative groups considered in the present chapter are
limited to those which form a fresh triad (or seventh or ninth),
temporarily replacing a basic one, and associated with it as an
auxiliary or an appoggiatura chord.

In classical harmony each of the notes of such a group was
directly related by step to its respective harmony notes.  The
movement of the parts maintained the connexion with basic
harmony, especially when the steps were all semitones.  Ex. 18
shows some movements, *a*, *c*, *e*, *g*, *h*, which are normal in
classical practice, and others which do not so strictly conform.
The B major triad in Ex. 18, although foreign to the key of
C, is thus easily available as a decoration, as is also the upper
auxiliary chord of D flat major.  The function of the semitone
in leading melodically to its following harmony note is clearly
evident in those cases, and the C tonality is not disturbed.  If
whole-tone and semitone steps are mixed, to produce auxiliary
chromatic chords, as at *b*, this leading effect is correspondingly weakened and the foreign chord assumes a more distinct
character.  Similarly, among diatonic auxiliary chords, the
link provided by part-movement facilitates association with the

Ex. 19  RAVEL 'Noctuelles' from *Miroirs*

Music extracts reprinted by permission of Schott & Co. Ltd.

Ex. 20  RAVEL 'Alborada del Gracioso' from *Miroirs*

Music extract reprinted by permission of Schott & Co. Ltd.

basic harmony. Compared with *c* the E minor chord in *d* emerges much more clearly as a definite change of harmony. There are many available shades of colour, and some subtly differing factors which control their use.  At Ex. 18*e* the note C is common to the two chords and acts as a pivot; at *f* there is similarly a pivot note, A, but a much more decisive chord change, partly through the remote relation of D minor and F sharp minor, partly through the presence of an assertive perfect fifth between the outside parts. At *g* there is an enharmonic link; at *h* the note E flat remains, as a seventh in the auxiliary chord; and at *i* a seventh is added to the root C.

Decorations of this kind were increasingly used by the nineteenth century romantic composers. The significant step is taken when these points of colour exist in their own right and are not strictly linked to the basic tonal progression. Loosening of the links can occur in two ways: by relaxing the note-to-note association demanded in classical part-writing, and by choosing decorative chords of more remote key relationship.

Ex. 19(*a*) shows the traditional way of relating each appoggiatura directly to its harmony note, on a basic chord of the ninth in this case. The example at *b* shows a chordal appoggiatura group (seen in its simple form at *c*) presented with less immediate note-by-note relation to its basic G chord, and with a tendency to exploit the separate character of the decorative chord. This device for giving a new flavour to quite orthodox decoration is obviously applicable to other chords besides simple triads or sevenths, and it needs to be taken into account in analysis of all twentieth century music, above all in piano music.

The second way of loosening relationship between decoration and its basic harmony, by choosing more remote auxiliary chords, is illustrated in Ravel's *Alborada del Gracioso*. In the opening bars the modern method of juxtaposition is used; this will be discussed in Chapter 6. But in the section beginning at bar 31, of which the first bar is quoted in Ex. 20(*a*), the procedure is virtually traditional except for the choice of decorative chords which have a clear identity as chords belonging to extraneous keys. An additional piquancy is given by friction against a pedal, a notable feature of Ravel's style. For convenience of comparison, several examples are brought to a common denominator at *b* and shown in simplified form in relation to C major.

An extension of the classical use of the appoggiatura should be observed. The cadence at Ex. 21*a* brings into apparent false relation the notes E flat and E natural; it is recognized in classical practice as a minor thirteenth followed by a *Tierce de Picardie*, or more directly, the E flat is an appoggiatura to the note D elliptically omitted. At *b*, the appoggiatura shown in brackets is a familiar decoration of the minor ninth A flat, but at *c* the A flat is elided and the resulting false relation is one which was not absorbed into classical harmony but which has become a commonplace in the twentieth century. The quotation at Ex. 22 from Ravel's *Scarbo* shows its use at 1, with its resolution omitted.

**Ex. 21**

**Ex. 22 RAVEL** *Scarbo*

Music extract reprinted by permission of Durand & Cie.

## *Structural Juxtapositions*

As decorative groups become increasingly separated from their parent harmony, the tendency towards complete freedom of juxtaposition among basic chords themselves is strengthened. The influence of decorative development thus reinforces the trend of the nineteenth-century harmony, which was towards greater flexibility in chord relations. The romantic composers

Ex. 23 WAGNER *The Valkyrie*

WAGNER *Siegfried*

Ex, 24 VAUGHAN WILLIAMS No.1 of *Five Mystical Songs*

Music extract reprinted by permission of Stainer & Bell Ltd.

used this freedom for expressive and descriptive purposes. In Ex. 23(*a*) is seen the 'sleep' motive from *The Valkyrie*, and at *b* the *Wanderer* motive from *Siegfried*. In both cases, the common or traditional relationships of the triads are avoided

and tonality is deliberately obscured for dramatic effect. Ex.
24 shows the extent to which such exceptional harmonic effects
have become normal practice. There is here no conscious
suspension of tonality; the triads, which would formerly have
been considered unrelated, from the standpoint of key- and
root-progression, are taken as normal harmonic colours, not
as chromatic departures from a diatonic norm. They are
brought into relation by the broad contrary motion of the two
main strands in the texture, not by root-relations.

In this way a difference of character emerges in the twentieth-
century use of chordal juxtaposition. The new use involves a
loosening of relations between basic triads and their tonal
centre, which corresponds to the loosening discussed above
between decorations and the basic triad. Just as appoggiatura
chords have been seen to throw off their note-to-note relationship with their harmony notes, now the triads shed their root-
to-root relationships, which gave a dominating position to the
primary triads in the establishing of a key.

Ex. 25 shows the harmonic basis of a section of the second
movement of Ravel's String Quartet, starting from bar 51.
The passage begins and ends on the dominant chord of A
minor, and shows traditional and modern progressions, and
some which are intermediate.

(a) 'Orthodox' movement occurs in bars 4 to 6, where the
chords have dominant-tonic relation, and there is an established modulation.

(b) The same interval relationship unites bars 2 and 3,
but with the heightened colour given by inflexion of the second
chord to F sharp. This augmented fourth root progression is
one of the commonest innovations in the transition stage.
By completely disrupting the primary triad organization and
using the chord farthest removed from the tonic, it lends
itself to external, descriptive effects, as in music associated with
the Wizard in Holst's *Perfect Fool*, or in the suggestion of the
dual nature of the puppet in Stravinsky's *Petrushka*. Its influence in the melodic field (see bars 2 and 3), was equally revolutionary. Comparison with Ex. 26b, where the original statement of bars 2 and 3 occurs, shows the effect of this influence.

Ex. 25 RAVEL String Quartet, second movement, bar 51
(Harmonic Basis)

Music extracts reprinted by permission of Durand & Cie.

Ex. 26 RAVEL Sonatine

RAVEL String Quartet, second movement
(Harmonic Basis)

DEBUSSY String Quartet, first movement

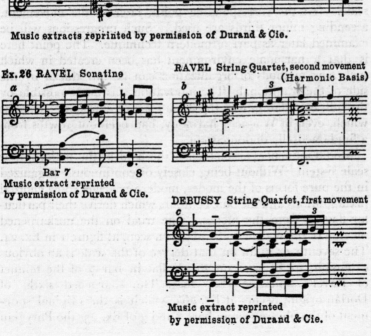

Bar 7    8
Music extract reprinted
by permission of Durand & Cie.

Music extract reprinted
by permission of Durand & Cie.

(c) Progression by roots a third apart was well established in classical, and more noticeably in romantic harmony (see Ex. 23a and b), but any chromaticism so introduced was normally resolved back into the diatonic scheme. The juxtapositions at bars 1, 2, and 6, 7, in Ex. 25 have only the loosest relation to any diatonic key; they suggest rather a free interplay of opposing chromatic inflexions, the connecting link being provided by a note common to the two chords.

(d) An extension of this common-note technique occurs in bars 7 to 11, where the upper D is seen as the fifth, the thirteenth, and the seventh, in the successive chords. Such flexibility of association follows naturally from the increased use of sevenths, ninths, etc., and encourages a greater freedom of juxtaposition. The introduction to the slow movement of the same quartet shows a more fully developed example.

(e) The final, completely modern method of progression is seen in bars 11 to 17. It is a pattern movement, ascending major thirds in the bass being set against the descending twelve-note scale. (At the corresponding point, later in the movement, ascending minor thirds are used.) Such progressions will be examined later as part of modern technique. The point here is that a harmonic environment has been created in which such new methods of organization can be introduced by the side of the traditional. The innovation was made possible by the full assimilation into the basic scale of chromatic elements which, even in Wagner's harmony, had been outgrowths from a fundamentally diatonic stem.

Modal influences also loosened the hold of the major-minor scale system. Without being closely or continuously organized in the pure forms of the modes, modern passages show chordal juxtapositions and melodic contours which derive their particular flavour from the modes. The triad on the unsharpened seventh of the scale has already been seen, at figure 1 in Ex. 24. The seventh or ninth on that degree of the scale is an obvious extension, to be seen on the E flat in bar 7 of the minuet of Ravel's Sonatine (Ex. 26a). The sharpened sixth, of Dorian origin, occurs at Ex. 26b, which is the original statement of the phrase seen in bars 2 and 3 of Ex. 25; the Phrygian mode is recalled in the opening of Debussy's Quartet (Ex. 26c). In this quasi-modal harmony, root relations generally follow traditional procedure, but the range of available notes is further extended, this time by reversion to some resources excluded from the classical method.

The cadence, whose dominant-tonic form is one of the most stereotyped features of classical harmony, is the natural point at which experiments and modifications occur. The three types of root progression used in Ex. 25, moving by fifths, by thirds, or by step, are available, with varied possibilities in chromatic inflexion and in use of triads, seventh, or ninths.   Another

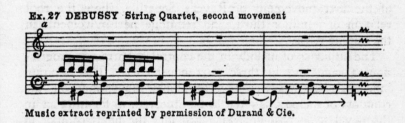

Ex. 27 DEBUSSY String Quartet, second movement

Music extract reprinted by permission of Durand & Cie.

RAVEL 'Alborada del Gracioso' from *Miroirs*

Music extract reprinted
by permission of Schott & Co. Ltd.

RAVEL Sonatine

Music extract reprinted by permission of Durand & Cie.

kind of cadential progression, or alternatively, of linking between sections, is illustrated in Ex. 27, where the leading effect of the semitone is employed, with emphasis on part-movement rather than on chordal relation. Ex. *a* shows a return to the main subject in G, made by semitone descent from the indeterminate tritone interval. Reference to the previous context will show that this is not a chordal resolution, but a semitone pivoting on the note G sharp. The same device is used by Ravel in the upward semitone movement at *b*. The transference of semitone resolution from one part to another is present between the first two chords at Ex. 27*c*. The last two chords in that example, which form the cadence of the first movement of Ravel's Sonatine, show the root relation of a minor third, and semitone part-movements in the middle parts.

The influence of melody in the control of harmonic progression is suggested in these part-movements. The opposite influence, that exercised by harmonic innovations on the contours of melody, is often to be observed, as for instance in the novel scale passage which provides the final scamper in Debussy's *Danse de Puck*, reflecting the juxtaposition of the chords of A flat and E. Nevertheless, it is essential, if a logical thread of progression is to be maintained, that the individual harmonic units should be given coherent direction. In transitional music which retains harmonic features of diatonic origin and association, this direction will be secured by melodic contours generally following traditional outlines. This broad tendency is obvious in Ex. 25, where the whole passage moves securely within the orbit of the tonality of A, in spite of the harmonic innovations which it incorporates.

On the other hand, as the diatonic is superseded by the twelve-note scale, new methods of tonal organization appear. One of the problems of twentieth-century composition is to find appropriate ways of relating the twelve available semitones of the octave, both harmonically and melodically, so that they are no longer merely decorations on an underlying diatonic framework. Meanwhile, compromise between traditional and non-traditional procedure is effected by frequent use of pedal-points; by notes retained and incorporated under new aspects in successive chords; and by basses moving in perceptible patterns, the most obvious consisting of semitone or whole-tone steps.

# CHAPTER FOUR

# DECORATION

## I

D ECORATION is as old as music itself, and probably older than any professionally cultivated form of the art. It appears in its essential form as a heightening of melodic intensity in plainsong, in the improvisations characteristic of Indian music, or in the embellishments of Hungarian Gipsy music. Combination of melodies, and the consequent evolution of harmony, brought melody under chordal domination in the classical phase of European music. Since the classical heritage supplies the bulk of the average listener's repertory, the close relation of melody to a fairly limited scheme of harmonies conditions his musical response. Nevertheless he has come to accept increasingly flexible relations of melody to its basic harmony, and can view with tolerant superiority his ancestors' violent reactions against a Wagner or a Strauss for what he now sees to be their enlargements of traditional scope. In characteristic twentieth-century music, however, melody has re-asserted much of its original independence, not only of the familiar classical chords but of any chordal scheme at all. The part played by decoration in that process of liberation is twofold. Decoration, as its name would imply, is either the ornamentation of a structure which could have a separate existence in plain form, or it may contribute melodic movements which are themselves an integral part of the structure. The Gipsy cadential embellishments are in the first category; the melismata of plainsong are in the second. The latter, as unaccompanied melody, is free to develop its own character in a manner not possible in the classical system, which requires clear definition of chord and key in order to secure the formal design of whole movements. For that purpose, decorative melodic features had to be strictly related to harmonic foundations.

Decoration played its part during the nineteenth century in loosening some of the rigidity of that basic chordal scheme, notably in Wagner's appoggiatura style. The process was quickened at the end of the century, and instead of being merely a ripple on the 'surface of harmony', it contributed to the revolution which was displacing the triad as the normal basic unit. Separate aspects of this general evolution can be examined in turn, though, like all transitional phenomena, they did not appear in successive historical stages but with overlapping and interaction. Firstly, the traditional practice of relating melodic lines to a preconceived chordal progression is continued, but with increased complexity and discord, and with increased freedom of melody from obvious harmonic association. Secondly, the modern preoccupation with the intrinsic interest of sounds leads to the cultivation of groups which originate from decorative processes but acquire a separate character of their own; they become established either as new self-subsisting chord shapes or are exploited as temporary empirical combinations for their own quality and sonority. Thirdly, in its horizontal aspect, decoration initiates part-movements which themselves produce the basic harmony and control the progression from chord to chord.

Developments of the traditional view of decoration are discussed in the present chapter, and the two more modern aspects in Chapter Five.

### Increased Complexity

One aspect of decoration was seen in Chapter Three, where auxiliary and appoggiatura movements produced fresh groups which were themselves recognizable as chords, in juxtaposition to the basic chord. The true view of decoration, as opposed to juxtaposition, is that the basic chord is maintained, but has one or more of its constituent notes temporarily displaced, and the resulting group is not separately identified as any traditional chord. The decorative devices are passing-notes, auxiliary notes, appoggiaturas, and suspensions, and distinction is made between accented and unaccented forms, single and multiple, diatonic and chromatic.

Expansion of the basic chordal resources has already been observed in Chapters One and Two to include whole-tone chords, sevenths, ninths, elevenths, and thirteenths as chords in their own right. The latter may be said to owe their origin to decorative processes, but they have become fully absorbed as individual chords. The material available to form the chord basis is therefore more complex and various than in normal classical harmony, and even without resort to innovation in decorative method itself, there is a wider scope for new harmonic richness and sonority. Experiment in this direction did not cease even when more distinctively modern methods had become established. Among the latter, parallelism and pattern progressions, for instance, often occur together with decoration as means of contributing to, and controlling, complex chromatic textures. The works of the composers quoted in this chapter and the next reveal these composite and overlapping styles.

Longer stretches of decoration over one chord can give a measure of sophistication to a simple basis, as in Ex. 28. The

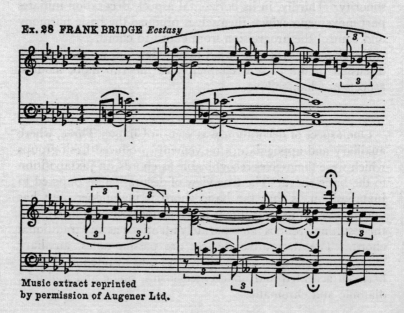

Ex. 28 FRANK BRIDGE *Ecstasy*

Music extract reprinted
by permission of Augener Ltd.

basic chord, a dominant seventh in second inversion, appears at
bar 2 in the left hand, its shape being anticipated by the
appoggiaturas in the first bar.  On this basis, a double strand

Ex. 29 FRANK BRIDGE *Bittersweet*

Music extracts reprinted by permission of Boosey & Hawkes Ltd.

of decoration in the right hand weaves around the notes of the
dominant ninth, eleventh, and thirteenth (the F flat in bar 1 is

D

an appoggiatura to the ninth, E flat); the full thirteenth chord unfolds in the fourth bar, with chromatic flattening of its fifth (to A double flat) and its thirteenth (to B double flat), leading to resolution in bar 5.

The textures evolved in piano writing, from Chopin and Liszt onwards, contribute to complexity of style and to the obscuring of the separate identity of 'voices' in a part-progression. (Contrast Ex. 19*b* with *c*.) Decorative devices absorbed into such texture may have little immediate connexion with their basic harmony notes; they may ultimately resolve, but at a different pitch, or at a later stage after other notes have intervened. Much of Scriabin's early piano work shows the style, with decorative discords entwined in Chopinesque figuration but with an increased abstruseness of resolution. Some further points are suggested by Ex. 29(*a*).

(*a*) The single line of semiquavers in the first two bars can be regarded as a broken-chord progression, with passing-note decoration of a basic C major chord, as indicated in Ex. 29*b*.

(*b*) Continuing the chordal interpretation, bar 3 (as shown in Ex. 29*c*) illustrates the process of assimilation of decoration into basic harmony: the A natural is an appoggiatura to the minor ninth on the root F sharp, and its resolution (the G in brackets) is elided. This form of ellipsis has been seen already (Ex. 21*c*), in an auxiliary-note movement. Here, in Ex. 29, it is embodied in the chord. From being a passing discord in classical use, it has become virtually a cliché among modern harmonic resources. It is often referred to as a 'false relation'; the term is a handy one to recall this particular device, though it is not strictly accurate in this connexion.

(*c*) Bars 3 and 5, Ex. 29*a*, should be compared. The right-hand figure is set in varied relation to two different roots, F sharp in the first case, and A in the second, and each note takes on a new aspect in analysis. The penultimate D sharp, for instance, is the thirteenth of the chord in bar 3, but in bar 5 it is an auxiliary with a loose relation to its harmony note E.

(*d*) This octave transposition of parts of a melodic progression is one of the factors contributing to the extended range, angularity, and character of modern melody. The tame re-arrangement of the original notes of bar 5 which appears at Ex. 29*d* shows the extent to which the character of melody can depend on the contours of figuration.

(*e*) As opposed to the above chordal interpretation, another approach may be made to the analysis of Ex. 29*a*. The shape of the three-note figure under the square bracket in bar 1 is maintained throughout the piece, and its stamp is imposed on the harmony. This choice of shapes and sounds for their intrinsic interest, and for their determining effect on harmony itself, is discussed in Chapter Five. Here we need only observe one of the technical means of achieving such consistent shapes, by varying the relation of figuration to its basic harmony and including decoration as part of a flexible texture. The suggestion of cross-rhythm in this three-note semiquaver figure set against the four-semiquaver background of two-four time also helps to contribute to this flexibility.

No attempt will be made to illustrate all the remaining nuances of decoration in the same detail. Composite clusters produced by decorative means abound in the lavish styles of the first decades of this century. Temporary bunchings of notes due to simultaneous decoration of more than one note of a chord; pedal notes and pedal chords; suggestions of bitonal effect as in Ravel's *Valses Nobles et Sentimentales*, No. 7 (see Ex. 115*c*); attraction of melody into relation with these incidental decorations and away from the basic chord; all these devices produce novelty of sound, yet analysis in many cases reveals a triad structure as the ultimate foundation of the harmony. It is enough to say that processes which began as momentary relaxings of chordal relations lead to the emergence of increasingly novel harmonic combinations, and to the acceptance of the idea of free flights of melody, often long sustained, and often travelling far from the orbit of any controlling chordal basis. The process ends, in fact, in a reversal of classical procedure, and in the development of musical texture as a web of independent melodic lines.

In attempting analysis of complex textures, alternative approaches must be borne in mind. For instance, it is not always possible to decide whether certain notes in a context are to be viewed as essential components of a thirteenth chord, or whether they are freely quitted decorative notes. The types of harmony evolved in transition from an already developed system, often with overlapping of old and new, must necessarily elude strict classification. The very elements which constitute the musical essence are the ones which cannot have an exact counterpart in words, in any style or period of music. The elements however which go to define the convention within which the composer's thoughts and intuitions move have importance both for the composer and the listener, and these can be separated by systematic study. If the lines of such study cross and overlap to some extent, they nevertheless bring the student nearer to an understanding of the composer's problem and its solution. With this object, a general classification of method is being suggested here, as a way of approach to analysis of twentieth-century works. The futility of dogmatism is stressed particularly in a period when harmony was rapidly absorbing into its basic fabric features which had formerly been definable as 'unessential' and supplementary.

### Greater Degree of Discord

There is no absolute standard of dissonance. The degree of discord which can be accepted has varied with different periods and with different people. Against the background of the accepted conventions of a period, a discord in the technical sense is a departure from the currently held idea of concord. In the days of Organum, intervals other than the perfect ones were unacceptable as concords; in the field of classical (academic) harmony, sound combinations other than triads are technically discords. As such, they are used for specific aesthetic purposes. Decoratively, they may contribute to grace and subtlety of melodic contour; in contrapuntal texture they may arise from the interplay of individual lines; above all, they further the onward propulsion of music from point to point in time, by the accumulation of tension and its subsequent release.

These aesthetic purposes have been served, against constantly changing backgrounds, as more complex sound combinations have been absorbed into the basic material of music. Up to the period of modern transition, each fresh accession of discord was assimilated as being related to an underlying chordal basis which possessed stability as an abstract conception in itself. Objection was not to dissonance itself. Far from it. The history of harmony could well be told as a preoccupation with discord, an endless exploring of its resources for expressive and for structural purposes. But within the closely defined convention of classical harmony, the limitations imposed upon discord were designed to prevent harmonic ambiguity which might obscure the logical basis.

If, however, the tonal scheme of music ceases to depend for its organization on root-progressions and clear identity of chord and key, and if other systems of organization are evolved as alternatives, there is no need for discords to be resolved or related to basic identifiable chords. So long as the sequence of musical thought is maintained by some valid method, the new convention can replace that of the triad which provided the foundation of classical harmony. An ascending scale harmonized by chords represents the classical convention; an ascending scale accompanied by a descending one involves momentarily a new convention, which depends on the recognition of a pattern of progression; any passing discord is readily accepted since the sequence of the musical thought is clearly presented by the pattern.

The basic materials of transitional harmony have already been seen to have a complex and varied character, and to derive from the desire to discover new shapes and sonorities. Several new conventions have become established in place of the former norm, and it is against these new backgrounds that the quality of discord must now be assessed. The old aesthetic purposes can still be fulfilled: decoration, interplay of melodic lines, tension and relaxation, all have their function as before but at a different level of concord. In this sense dissonance keeps the same relative position as it held in the past.

There is however one new aspect. The search for new sonorities found one of its outlets in exploiting discord as a sensation in itself. It was welcomed for its own interest, not just tolerated as an unavoidable concomitant of expanded resources. Some of the ways of indulging this newly acquired taste for the flavour of discords may be examined.

Attention can be focused on dissonance by the spacing of chords to bring the sharpest discords, such as major sevenths and minor seconds and ninths into prominence, a divergence from classical practice only in the matter of emphasis, but none the less indicative of the changing norm of consonance, and allowing old resources to be used in new ways. Ex. 30a, from Ravel's String Quartet, shows a very pointed arrangement of the thirteenth chord on E flat, at figure 1, in marked contrast with the traditional arrangement of the chord at b which occurs two bars earlier. The second bar of a, with its appoggiaturas at 2 and 3, represents approximately the limit of dissonance acceptable in classical harmony.

Friction, produced by consecutive discords when part-movement takes place, is no new experience; but the extent to which it affects the essential structure of harmony, as opposed

Ex. 30 RAVEL String Quartet, first movement

Music extracts reprinted by permission of Durand & Cie.

to its acceptance when strongly individual lines of melody
make temporary clashes, is a matter of style. When he learns
the average classical procedure through academic practice,
the student is advised to avoid such movements. In contrast,
two stages in the emergence of modern style are shown in Ex.
31. The seventh to the ninth in the outside parts at *a*, in a

Music extracts reprinted by permission of Boosey & Hawkes Ltd.

harmonic texture which has absorbed seventh and ninth
chords and their decorations as basic material, calls for no
comment, but the use of the ninth to seventh in the two upper
parts at *b* shows a deliberate choice of this friction as a point
of harmonic colour.

The use of a decorative note simultaneously with the
harmony note it is supposed to replace is also prohibited in
academic theory, except when the harmony note is in the bass;
this is partly for the sake of clarity of chord-structure and
identity, partly owing to the stage of evolution reached in
normal classical acceptance of discord. Also in the interest of
clarity, the clash of decorative notes against one another
was not a usual practice. (It should be recalled, however,
that before the formalizing of harmony in the 'galant' style
and the Viennese sonata period, the works of J. S. Bach
abounded in such clashes, arising from the overriding vigour
of his melodic and contrapuntal lines.) The relaxing of these
prohibitions is not merely a licence; it follows naturally when a
narrow view of the triad convention is replaced by a wider one.

Discord increases as semitones are included in the groupings.

Diatonic clusters like those seen earlier in Exs. 6 and 7 have
what is virtually a neutral effect; some chromatic appoggiatura
combinations are readily acceptable by having a recognizable
chordal shape in themselves, and consequent association with
familiar harmony, as in Ex. 32a; no difficulty is presented by
piquant placings of pedal notes (Ex. 32b) since the context
gives explanation of the discord.

Ex.32 WARLOCK *Rest, Sweet Nymphs*     RAVEL Sonatine

Music extract reprinted by          Music extract reprinted
permission of the publishers,        by permission of Durand & Cie.
Oxford University Press.

As opposed to such conjunctions of decorative and harmony
notes which have a certain degree of stability, there are others
which are designed expressly to give a sharp edge to decorative
movements against a background, to add a quality of acerbity
to what may be quite a simple basis; cf. the clashing horn parts
of Ex. 32, from the Walton Symphony. As transitional experiments exhausted their impetus and positive re-orientations
were made, simplicity was sought in contrast to the excessive

Ex. 33 WALTON Symphony, first movement.

Music extract reprinted by permission of the publishers, Oxford
                                           University Press.

complexity of the earlier, transitional period. One function of discord, which was developed during that transition, was to contribute to this simplification of texture, since it provided (e.g. in the simultaneous use of the major and minor third in bars 2 and 3 of Ex. 33), a means of giving new relations and new significance to familiar things.

CHAPTER FIVE

# DECORATION
## II

T HE VIEW OF DECORATION now to be taken involves a
broadening of definition. In its narrowest form, the
word implied an ornamentation of an already established
chord, but in its new aspect, decoration has a structural function; it is not simply an element which is temporarily added,
but it is rather a process of transformation and new creation.
In varying degrees it retains something of its original meaning,
and while producing new chordal shapes it reveals the connexion of those shapes with a separately conceived generating
harmonic basis. The influence of chordal harmony on musical
texture prevails inasmuch as that original meaning is retained,
and is weakened as the idea of decoration becomes one of
melodic movement rather than superficial ornament. The
static view of harmony then gives place to one which allows
a freer play of horizontal lines, and at that point the idea of
chordal decoration ceases to be relevant. There are many
stages to examine before the final contrapuntal position is
reached, and in this transitional phase the influence of
decorative movements on harmony is still relevant. It will
be discussed in relation firstly to chord structure, and secondly
to chord progression.

### Chord Structure

Passing reference has already been made to the arrangement
of decorative features designed to bring out new flavours of
harmony, and to the production of whole-tone chords by
decorative movements. An example of the latter process can
be seen in the passage beginning twenty bars from the end
of the first movement of Debussy's String Quartet. Ex. 34a,

at the beginning of the Rigaudon in Ravel's *Tombeau de Couperin*
is, technically, no more than a decorative progression of
passing-notes in the bass added to a major seventh chord on
the root C (which is itself produced by the passing note movement shown at 34*b* and retained as a pedal). The passage
owes its particular harmonic quality to the diatonic clusters
on the crotchet beats.

Ex. 34 RAVEL 'Rigaudon' from *Le Tombeau de Couperin*

Music extracts reprinted by permission of Durand & Cie.

The following example, No. 35, shows the same principle
at work, in various stages of complexity. At *a*, the notes
E flat, E, F, G, joined by lines, have a decorative relation,
by auxiliary and passing-notes, to a basic G minor chord.
In the next stage, at *b*, the changing-note figure under the
bracket at 1 is carried on from the end of the first verse of
the voice part and its F sharp is incorporated into the rocking
accompaniment figure at 2. The end of the second verse
contributes an inverted dominant pedal, a fifth D-A, to
enrich the harmony of the rocking figure, and the process

Ex. 35 WARLOCK *Cradle Song*

Music extracts reprinted by permission of the publishers, Oxford
University Press.

of amplification continues to the end of the song, the chords owing their structure to the auxiliary-note movement which has prevailed throughout.

The part played by decoration in these examples is clearly more than an ornamental one; it leads to the presence of sound combinations of quite new quality throughout the song. Groups emerge which still have their origin in triad harmony, but whose shapes and sonorities take on separate character as basic materials of harmony. When such groups are accepted as separate chordal entities, and not as modifications of an abstract normal structure built up by thirds from a root, there is a new principle at work. A new one, yet an old one. Just as harmony came into being as a development of the vertical cross-sections of previous contrapuntal textures, its sound-combinations being snapshots as it were of the attitudes achieved by music in action, so the harmony of the twentieth century transition is a vertical view of sounds which occur simultaneously in time, but against a more complicated and discordant background of movement. The parallel with the past occurs in the 'freezing' of music in action; the difference from the past, apart from heightened discord, is that this action, instead of resulting from free melodic movements as in early polyphony, takes the form of decorative movements on an established chordal basis. A triad monopoly had been created in the homophonic period, and transitional music had the double problem of breaking that monopoly and of drawing on the store of living movements growing out of it, in order to extend the range of chordal choice. If that choice, in any period, becomes stereotyped, and any convention of basic harmony is adopted as a norm, there is practical advantage in ease of understanding, but there is corresponding disadvantage in the tendency to ossification.

Assuming that a decorative group (e.g. the appoggiatura chord at 1 in Ex. 36a), is displacing a basic triad, its shape may be retained and so acquire a separate harmonic status. In the case of this quotation from the third of Frank Bridge's *Three Poems*, the underlying B chord is never sounded in its plain form; the heightened colour of its decorative substitute is employed for five consecutive bars. It will be noticed that the right-hand group at fig. 1 is the familiar appoggiatura decoration of a diminished seventh chord, possessing a little more tang than that well-worn combination, but well on the way to becoming just as much a cliché. The obvious resolution is avoided, in the progression from 2 to 3. The latter group, as used in this piece, illustrates both the traditional and the modern attitude to composite chords. Here, the 'orthodox'

Ex. 36 FRANK BRIDGE *Sunset*

Music extracts reprinted by permission of Augener Ltd.

resolution is shown, to the E minor triad at 4. The newer
way of thought appears at the opening of the piece, shown in
Ex. 36*b*. Resolution to the assumed harmony notes in brackets
is omitted. Moreover, the group at 2 is then taken as a starting
point (figure 3 in Ex. 36*c*) for a pattern progression, and so
passes into basic harmony.

The same principle accounts for the common practice of
retaining decorative groups at final cadences and allowing
them to fade away without resolution (see Ex. 6). Its influence is exerted not only on the general colour and content of
harmony, but on the way of thinking about music in its fluid
rather than in its static aspect.

Anticipation of a decorative group has the same effect of
contributing to new harmonic standards. The major seventh
chord at the opening of Frank Bridge's *Fragrance* (Ex. 37*a*),
makes six appearances before providing its own technical
explanation in a perfectly orthodox resolution to the ninth
chord on G (Ex. 37*b*). The long anticipation has permitted a

Ex. 37  FRANK BRIDGE  *Fragrance*

Music extracts reprinted by permission of Boosey & Hawkes Ltd.

new range of colours to be opened up. As a natural corollary,
the standard of harmony which is established there will be a
fair indication of the average for the whole piece. Consistency
of style demands that there should be homogeneity both in the
subject-matter and in its manner of presentation.

The maintenance of consistency depends on a true estimate
of what are stable groupings, capable of separate existence as
harmonic units, and what are heightenings of tension in relation
to those units. Stability is not meant to imply any particular

degree of acceptable discord measured by an absolute standard. Gradations of discord certainly do exist among sounds considered separately as intervals: the minor second and ninth and the major seventh are more acute than the major second and ninth and the minor seventh. If an abstract system of harmony were being constructed, those facts would assume more importance than they do at the present stage of this study, which is concerned with transition from already estab- lished practice.* The test of stability which is proposed here, during the course of evolution to fully modern method, is that of intelligibility through association with what is already established in harmonic experience.

The appoggiatura groups shown in Ex. 38 entered into harmony as decorations controlled by part-movement; they belong to an early stage in the assimilation of discord. Broadly classified, these appoggiatura groups:

(*i*) combine with a note, or notes, of the basic chord to form a recognizable chord preceding the main one; that is, to form a juxtaposition in the manner of Chapter Three. Ex. 38 *a* to *e* illustrates the formation in this way of a triad, a diatonic seventh chord, an augmented sixth chord, a seventh chord in a foreign key, and a whole-tone chord.

(*ii*) form a recognizable chord shape superimposed on the basic one. Ex. 38 *f* to *i* shows a dominant seventh, a dominant thirteenth, a chromatic triad, a chromatic seventh chord (more obvious if A flat is read enharmonically as G sharp), superimposed in turn on a C major triad; and at *j*, a dominant seventh chord decorating an underlying diatonic seventh. Such combinations arose easily in traditional practice in the form of pedal harmony. The cohesion among the separate groups, arising from close spacing and from familiar chordal associations, contributes greatly to the stability of the total combination in each of these cases.

---

*They are in fact taken into account in Krenek's *Studies in Counterpoint*, 1940, in his presentation of the Twelve-Note System, and in Hindemith's *Craft of Musical Composition* (English translation 1948), which gives an exhaustive analysis of relations between sounds. The latter's classification of chords has many points of correspondence with harmonic theory based on historical evolution.

Against a background in which such examples have become average harmonic groups, increase of tension is to be looked for in combinations which show less obvious relation to triad foundations (Ex. 39).

Departure from classical principles by the sounding of decorations against harmony notes was seen in the previous chapter to lead to greater measures of discord, especially if semitones are present. Applying the test of association with familiar harmony, stability will be found in such cases to depend on the extent to which spacing clearly reveals a recognizable chord. If the chords at Exx. 39 *a* and *b* are compared, the second has a more familiar sound in relation to traditional harmony than the first, although it contains the more dissonant interval

C to B; and at *c*, the progression has the feeling of relaxing from tension, in spite of the move to the dissonant note B. The dominant harmony appearing at *b* and *c* makes itself more readily recognizable than the less clearly defined group at *a*. A similar comparison between *d* and *e* shows that the second chord has a dominant thirteenth in its customary position, superimposed on C, whereas the group at *d*, containing the same notes, has a spacing which recalls no harmonic association and emphasizes the dissonant minor ninth, E F.

Close grouping of notes in thirds obviously contributes to ease of triad identification, as at *f*, where a superimposed dominant ninth is evident. The clash of separate triads, however, may acquire prominence as at *g*, where there is a strong conflict between tonic and dominant harmony when the low E is added to complete the C chord. At *h* this conflict is not so apparent, since the B flat defines the whole group as a thirteenth chord on the root C.

Applying the same analysis in the case of one decoration clashing with another, Exx. 39 *i* to *n* show how the major seventh interval (or its equivalent, the diminished octave), which in itself is strongly discordant, can be assimilated into harmony in proportion as it brings with it recognizable associations. In the group at *i*, the diminished octave F sharp-F makes its full impact as a discord; at *j*, if read enharmonically as G flat, it is tempered by coalescing as part of a superimposed seventh chord. Used in relation to a basic seventh chord, the double decoration at *k* recalls the simpler decoration at *i*. Comparison of *m* and *n* reveals once more the blending effect of close spacing in thirds; the latter example, although adding the extra dissonance of the E - E flat interval, establishes itself the more readily because it embodies the common 'false relation' chord (cf. Ex. 36*a*).

The 'familiar harmony', which by its presence eases the process of decorative assimilation, has repeatedly taken the form of superimposed chords in Exs. 38 and 39; one part of a total combination has recognizable shape, not necessarily the whole. Variations both of harmonic colour and tension can be obtained by the different placings of these sub-groups in

E

relation to the full chord. Ex. 40 shows some simple re-orientations of a G major triad, which is seen first as part of various
chords, then as a decorative group in relation to other chords.
The quotations at Ex. 41 show the diminished octave interval,
produced by decorative movement, in different relations to
basic harmony.

Music extracts reprinted by permission of Durand & Cie

The static aspect of these shapes has so far been considered.
In the next section, emphasis will be on the progression from
one chord to another, but that process will be seen to have an
inevitable influence on chord structure itself.

## *Chord Progression*

The test of stability proposed above had reference to static sound groups considered in isolation. Something more than a chance and temporary conjunction of notes was looked for in a combination intended to have a separate harmonic status. If, however, an alternative explanation of a group in any context is clearly given by the logic of part-progression, there is no need for a purely harmonic test. The shapes produced in Ex. 42*a*, at 1 and 2, are normal decorations of basic triads, and the two inner lines of melody moving in contrary motion provide the logical continuity. There is consequently no difficulty in following the same thread at *b*, where the outward melodic movement produces the mixed group at 3, which is then kept for another twelve bars to the end of the piece and does not need any explanation of its structure other than that given by its origin in movement.

Ex. 42  BARTOK *Mikrokosmos* No. 122

Music extracts reprinted by permission of Boosey & Hawkes, Ltd.

Ex. 43 repeats the same process and arrives at its final group by an obvious contrary motion progression. This example is added not so much as a technical illustration, but to indicate a modern attitude. The final group makes no claim to be a stable harmonic entity; to resolve its appoggiaturas to their obvious G major destination would be as laboured as explaining a joke.  If allusions and half-statements can be taken up by the listener, music can bring within its sphere elements of wit and sophistication that it was not formerly expected to show.  The technical term for such half-statement,

Ex. 43  POULENC  Six Impromptus, No. 3

Music extract reprinted by permission of J. & W. Chester Ltd.

Ex. 44  WARLOCK  Sleep

Music extract reprinted by permission of the publishers, Oxford
University Press

ellipsis, has been used more than once; the prevalence of its use in transitional music is a measure of the increased demand which composers are making on the listener's intelligence and experience.

Ellipsis has so far been seen mostly in relation to single chords, in the form of decoration applied to a basis already established in a context.  Its use at the point of progression between chords was seen in Ex. 36a, from 2 to 3, though the chord at 2 had become so confirmed that it hardly contained any suggestion of omission. A continuous application of the device can be seen in *Solitude*, No. 1 of Three Poems by Frank Bridge, where successive changes of chord take place before the decorations applied to the previous chord have come to their resolution.

This is perhaps less a pointer to new methods of harmony, than a telescoping of features which have become obvious in older harmony; it implies a certain redundancy of decorative detail applied to some basis which can be thought of in the abstract. Its contribution to new harmonic experience lies in its avoidance of conventional shapes, in its increase of discord, and in the fact that it presupposes onward movement as the mainspring of the music; an ancient principle, but one which tended to recede in classical harmony.

The practical approach to the question of chord progression, as an alternative or supplement to specific choice of root relations, is to allow movement of the separate parts to produce empirical combinations which may or may not be analysable as traditional chord structures. The effect of this fluid contrapuntal method can be seen in Ex. 44, from the end of the song *Sleep*, by Peter Warlock. The first half of bar 1 consists of triad harmony with some decorative colouring, but from figure 1 to the end of the bar both the individual chord-shapes and the progression from one to another are determined by the chromatic part-movement. This quotation may be taken as an epitome of the process of transition from classical harmony. In its broad outline, it is a dominant-tonic cadence; in its decorative detail it shows traditional procedure up to figure 1, with triad outlines clearly preserved, and from that point increasingly obscured; it moves, as a result of these decorative movements, through a subsidiary chordal progression above the bracket at 2, producing a non-classical juxtaposition when it resolves to the final chord; and it illustrates, at 2, chord-shapes and a degree of discord which belong to a new era.

Progression from one chord to another may be either partially or wholly controlled by contrapuntal movement. Since this study is concerned first with tendencies within the established system of classical harmony, it is natural to expect that a considerable amount of traditional tonal organization will underlie many of the new shapes taken by decorative groups. Ex. 45*a* shows that a completely traditional chord-basis may be given new colour and modified shape by movements of parts which are scarcely more than new inflexions. The general framework of the tonic key and the chordal progression in E flat, which is suggested at *b*, is given subtle colouring by Warlock through part-movements which avoid explicit statements of chords in their normal key-relationships.

Ex. 46 is a sample of the superimposed chromaticism to which transitional harmony tended while it was still anchored to old tonal progressions. When the partial control of progression seen in Exx. 45 and 46 is removed, a state of harmonic fluidity is reached in which the need becomes apparent for alternative methods of securing relationships to a central tonic. Temporary suspension of control, between fixed tonal points, had been possible long before modern days: the extent to which this can bring with it extraneous tonal suggestions can be judged by Ex. 47, from a Mozart piano sonata. The

Ex.45  WARLOCK  *Sigh no more, ladies*

Music extract reprinted by permission of the publishers, Oxford
University Press

**Ex. 46 ROGER-DUCASSE Barcarolle No. 3**

Music extract reprinted by permission of Durand & Cie

progression across the double-bar, interpolated between a seventh chord in E flat and a diminished seventh in F minor, makes an unusual impact, since a move is made in all three parts at once to a chromatic decorative group remote from either key. Key definition is quickly restored in this case, and although such temporary passages of heightened colour grow longer and appear more frequently in the harmony of the romantic composers, return is equally made to a defined tonality. The same principle of temporary divergence can hold good in modern harmony, but with the added resources of new chordal shapes and qualities of discord. Experiment on the lines of Ex. 48 will show not only that part-movements can be made to lead chromatically far afield (*b*), but also be made to produce particular chordal shapes (*c* and *d*), or degrees of discord (*e*).

Ex. 49 shows an application of such method. It begins and ends at a fixed tonal point, in D flat; it owes both its chord-shapes and chord progressions to chromatic part-movement; and at the same time it illustrates two significant controlling factors in modern chromatic progressions (discussed later in Chapters Seven and Eight), parallel movement of parts in a

**Ex. 47 MOZART Piano Sonata in B flat, K 333, second movement**

chordal strand (*a*), and, more important in this case, the clearly perceptible pattern in the contrary-motion phrases in each bar and in the rising stepwise bass progression.

Ex.48

Ex. 49 BAX Toccata for Piano

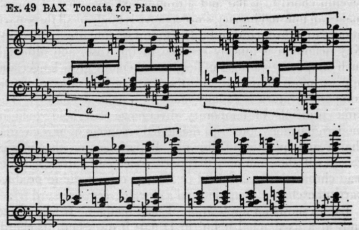

Music extract reprinted by permission of Chappell & Co. Ltd. London

We may well conclude this view of transition at a point where compromise is effected between old tonal demands and new ways of meeting them. The process so far considered has been one of evolution, not revolution, an expansion of former method rather than a substitution of new. The review has been carried well into the present century, ignoring for the moment procedures which imply a direct break with tradition, although they had begun to appear even before this century opened. But even without reference to those innovations, it is clear that the logical end of developments within classical technique is a final dissolution of the system itself. The triad comes to lose its dominance as the normal harmonic group to which all temporary shapes are ultimately related. It does so, partly through a new sensuous interest in sounds and their varied groupings, partly through new scale influences, and partly through complexity of decoration and elision of plain basic harmony. The major-minor scale environment, within which the triads were inter-related to define specific keys, is superseded either by fresh modal influences or by expansion to include all the twelve semitones as part of the normal scale. Most important of all, since movement is the essence of music, the static conception of a chordal type of harmony, which was developed in the seventeenth century and gave its stamp to classical melody, is replaced by a dynamic conception, in which the lines of melody have a dominating role in giving shape to harmony. The word harmony, in fact, has to be used in a very elastic way to interpret the musical phenomena of the twentieth century. It will continue, in Part Two, to refer in the normal way to sounds heard simultaneously; but the extent to which this will involve examination of horizontal movements is a measure of the distance which has been travelled from the abstract chord of the classical system.

# CHAPTER SIX

# SOME ASPECTS OF STYLE

I T HAS BEEN SUGGESTED that two different interpretations of the function of music could be made; one 'pure', and the other expressive. It was also suggested that Debussy's* sensitivity to new and varied experiences in sound was instrumental in turning music away from the excesses of romantic expressiveness to a new view of the potentialities of sounds themselves. This antithesis was admitted to be a 'drastic simplification'; and it was presented as a means of appreciating the motive force in the movement away from emotionally charged romanticism. In practice, at any rate outside the Neoclassic field, there is really a close interaction between these two functions of music. Musical resources, however purely they may originally be conceived, tend strongly to be used for descriptive and expressive purposes; and effects conceived for their striking and urgent character tend, through repetition and familiarity, to be absorbed into the general fund of technical material. Thus, although the modern spirit first revealed itself as a revolt against a system overgrown with complications, musical and extra-musical, it quickly developed complex processes of its own. Although Debussy revealed the beauties of pure colour, in so doing he made available a new palette for descriptive purposes and for a further externalization of music.

The key to processes of transition was found in the cult of sounds in fresh aspects instead of as parts of an established system. This criterion is still valid in modern works, but these

*The singling out of Debussy, here and in the Introduction, does less than justice to the influence of others like Chabrier, Fauré, and Satie, who helped in applying the essentially French antidote to romantic exuberance. That Gallic strain, to which they contributed as pioneers, has persisted amid the heterogeneous styles of this century, but it was Debussy who brought this spirit to a focus in specific technical form.

new findings were quickly adopted as basic materials. Are these findings, then, to take their place in one composite technique, forming a background against which further innovations will stand in relief? That is to say, has the composer necessarily to adopt the full gamut of twelve semitones as his working basis, and obtain his 'significant order' always in reference to them? Or are there to be selective principles? Is a more restricted basis to be adopted, a modal one for example? or some arbitrary selection from the available twelve semitones, the remaining resources being called upon as desired? Twentieth-century music includes styles varying from the uncompromising chromaticism of Schönberg's Twelve-Note system, to empirical choices by individual composers in individual works. No general norm exists as it did in the classical system. The most that can be said is that each composer can create his own norm, and achieve his contrasts by variations from that norm.

The musical purpose served by those varied relations to a norm is open to the double interpretation suggested above. Taking the 'pure' view of music, the principles by which melody, harmony, and rhythm are brought into a synthesis will not differ in essence from those of any other period of music, however different the ways in which they are applied. In the matter of external associations there is a much wider scope in modern music, with its greater variety of harmonic structure, colour, and intensity. The harmony of Debussy's *Pelléas et Mélisande* provides an apt example of this power of association, and of an economy of means achieved by deliberate selection. The work stands at the threshold of modern music; its norm is not far removed from triad harmony and its derivative sevenths and ninths, and it is therefore easy to assess the particular qualities and flavours of the newer resources employed. First with regard to whole-tone harmonies. The loose statement that Debussy is a 'whole-tone composer' is not supported by the facts, either in *Pelléas* or in the general body of his work. In the opera whole-tone harmonies form only a part of the total fabric, and when they do occur they have a specific association. It was seen in Chapter Two that these chords, considered purely technically, obscure tonality and produce vagueness of progression; and it is precisely in contexts in the opera where there is disturbance, either psychologically or in the physical environment that they are used. Their general function is differentiated from that of other chords, and there is considerable variety of texture within the whole-tone field itself. Ex. 50 shows a few of these many varied uses. At *a*, the opening bars of the work, whole-tone harmonies from bar 5 appear in full chordal form, reflecting, in sharp contrast with the prevailing diatonic background, the tense human relationships of the drama. Different textures occur at *b* and *c*. The placid character of *b*, associated with the secluded well in the park, owes much to the smooth blend of major thirds brought into prominence by the spacing, in contrast to the

Ex.50  DEBUSSY · *Pelléas et Mélisande*·

Music extracts reprinted by permission of Durand & Cie

Ex. 51 SCHÖNBERG *Pelléas et Mélisande*

Music extracts reprinted by arrangement with Universal Edition A.G. Vienna
(Alfred A. Kalmus, London)

uneasy whole-tone scale ostinato at *c* which persists while
Golaud and Pelléas are in the castle vaults. Examples *d* and
*e* illustrate one of the many psychological nuances underlined
by the restless character of whole-tone melody: the phrase at
*d* accompanies Golaud's anxious questioning of Mélisande,
but it settles into diatonic contours at *e*, where the pacified
Golaud attempts to console Mélisande.

The opposite extreme to this selective use of harmony is seen in Ex. 51, from Schönberg's tone-poem, *Pelléas et Mélisande*, based on the same play and appearing in the same year, 1902. Schönberg's opening, at *a*, has a whole-tone basis with appoggiatura additions, and at *b*, where whole-tone chords supply the harmony entirely, they do so as fully absorbed and normal material. Here the choice is in favour of full and equal use of the twelve semitones and of all available resources in a composite technique.

Brief illustration of the remaining transitional resources will show the same two opposing tendencies in style, the selective and the absorptive. The chordal juxtapositions discussed in Chapter Three were seen to lead logically to a complete chromaticism; but before that kaleidoscopic stage is reached, juxtapositions can be seen which still retain a functional use. Quoting again from Debussy's *Pelléas*, Ex. 52*a* conveys in musical terms a sharp break in the sequence of progression, which accompanies one of the inconsequent interruptions made by the child Yniold during jealous questioning. The eclectic approach is seen, on the other hand, at 52*b*, taken from Schönberg's second String Quartet, and 52*c*, from Hindemith's String Quartet Op. 10, both assuming as part of their basic harmony the free movement of chords between any scale degrees.

The new chord-shapes produced by added notes or by fresh spacings (more fully treated in Part Two as 'neutral' chords), do not occur frequently in *Pelléas*, but their few appearances are significant. First (Ex. 53*a*), where Yniold is trying to move a stone too big for him: 'It is heavier than the whole earth', he says: and second (53*b*), the undulating figure accompanying the scene of the flock of sheep.

Exx. 53*c* and *d* show one composer reacting in the two different ways. The first, from Bartok's opera *Bluebeard's Castle*, shows 'neutral' chords used in a descriptive way, as Judith gazes on the lake of tears, 'pale, still water'; and the second, from the end of the same composer's first String Quartet, shows the final chord as a completion of the melodic movement in the preceding bars, and so belonging to the logic of the music itself. In *Bluebeard's Castle* there is the same apt differentiation of harmonic types and flavours as in Debussy's *Pelléas*, though at a more advanced stage of technical development. Both works

Ex. 52 DEBUSSY *Pelléas et Mélisande*

Music extract reprinted by permission of Durand & Cie

SCHÖNBERG Second String Quartet, second movement

Music extract reprinted by arrangement with Universal Edition A.G. Vienna (Alfred A. Kalmus, London)

HINDEMITH String Quartet, Opus 10, second movement

Music extract reprinted by permission of Schott & Co. Ltd.

Ex.53 DEBUSSY ·Pelléas et Mélisande

Music extracts reprinted by permission of Durand & Cie

BARTOK  Bluebeard's Castle

c    Weis-ser stil-les    Wass - er seh' ich'

Music extract.reprinted by arrangement with Universal Edition (London) Ltd.

reveal the modern spirit in their sonorous qualities, the earlier virtually within the framework of tradition and the later completely within the newly established technique. It is only necessary to mention Stravinsky's pre-1914 ballets to call up a picture of the latest and most vivid stage in this early twentieth-century development of the descriptive power of music.

This double principle, the selective use of newly created harmonies and the absorption of resources into a basic stock, underlies traditional developments and runs on into the

BARTOK First String Quartet, third movement · ·

Music extract reprinted by arrangement with Universal Edition (London) Ltd.

modern movement which follows. Its technical outcome will be the subject of the second part of this study, and the method of approach will be, as in Part One, through the latent potentialities of the musical materials themselves, rather than through a historical examination of individual composers' work. The standard of reference will no longer be primarily the classical system of harmony. The principle will not be so much one of measuring deviations and effecting compromises with a parent stock, as of making fresh assessments of separate harmonic phenomena and of new ways of organizing them in a significant whole.

F

# PART TWO

## *MODERN METHODS*

ALTHOUGH the study of transition from traditional harmony has shown the emergence of some new tone-colours and suggested some of the potentialities which are inherent in the twelve-note scale, it might seem that these gains have been made only by sacrificing a working system which co-ordinated all the separate elements and gave them their several functions. A negative attitude has repeatedly prevailed, one which deliberately looked for signs and portents of disruption. To turn from this negative phase to a positive one it will be necessary to broaden the view and try to see the larger perspective within which the details of harmony are to be set.

The outstanding feature of European music has been the development of complex textures of simultaneous as well as successive sounds. The first, prevailingly contrapuntal phase was one in which strands of melody were so combined that each line of the texture preserved its individuality and yet maintained a certain degree of basic concord with the other lines. This degree of concord corresponded to that existing among the first six notes of the harmonic series. In the succeeding 'harmonic' phase there developed a more direct consciousness of the vertical combinations as units analysable apart from the horizontal lines of which they formed the cross sections. In both phases the basic idea was that of a texture in depth, a filling in of the space between an upper and lower line of melody, a treble and a bass. Whatever changes have taken place in the last thousand years of Western music, that principle has persisted, and it still persists in the twentieth century.

A further principle, characteristic of life itself, is that of alternating states of tension and repose. In music it has always existed, in the rise and fall of melody, in the impact of varying rhythms, in the mutual interplay of melody and rhythm; and finally, with increasing complexity as European music developed, in the frictions which can arise between simultaneous sounds. In both the phases referred to in the previous paragraph the simplest measure of the state of tension was to be found in the divergence of sound-combinations from the norm of concord existing among the first six notes of the harmonic series, in harmonic terms, the major or minor triad. Such divergence constituted discord, and this formed part of the nature of music itself. As long as the triad standard of concord prevailed, valid systems of harmony and counterpoint could be formulated which related all dissonances to that standard.

If the triad basis loses this position of pre-eminence what has the twentieth century to put in its place? Can the negative attitude, the mere revolt against the classical harmonic system, be replaced by a positive one? It can, if the broad perspective is kept and the triad is seen as the subsidiary feature that it was, a norm of reference within the larger framework of the two-part outlines. The position can then be restated in positive terms. Musical texture will continue to be bounded by an upper and lower line of melody. It will continue to reflect, in the interplay of its separate melodic, rhythmic, and harmonic elements, the rise and fall of tension inseparable from human experience; but in the detailed filling in of the two-part outline the triad criterion will be replaced by a much wider one. Any method of organizing the details of texture which has perceptible order and which contributes to the significance of the whole will be a valid technical resource.

It is a far cry from the triad system to 'any perceptible order'. Yet it is no greater than the gulf between our individual sensations of the world about us and the interpretation of that world given to us by the atomic physicist or the astronomer. The triad is of course included in the idea of 'perceptible order'. Being closest to the fundamental and uncomplicated ordering of sounds in nature, it conveys a sense of repose, negatively by the absence of friction and positively by reconciling in a unity the root and its fifth, the two strong poles among natural sounds. Its appeal to mind and to sense is the most balanced and satisfying. For this reason the triad norm of reference may well remain unchallengeable for ever in the domain which corresponds to man's direct and sentient relation to his environment. But when a scientist probes the structure and nature of the universe, he has to move on planes of thought which have little relation to his sentient existence. A composer similarly may move in regions of thought and intuition where the particular order of everyday life is irrelevant, where the sensuous satisfaction given by triads and their associated harmonies has nothing to do with his new music of the spheres. To approach this new world, the composer needs a technique not only widened in range but different in quality. If these abstract regions of thought are brought within the range of music, technical method must match the thought and the appeal will be increasingly to the listener's mind rather than to his feelings.

That is an extreme position, which may be touched in some phases but by no means in all. It is a measure of the great range of thought and technique which twentieth century music embraces. Two fully worked out systems have been advanced, one by Schönberg, one by Hindemith, to organize coherently the full resources of the twelve-note scale. On the other hand, Joseph Yasser reaches the conclusion* that with a scale of twelve semitones undifferentiated in function there can be no fundamental system of harmony but only *ad hoc* arrangements of sounds in each composition. Such a situation presents both a challenge and an opportunity to a composer. Each composition must establish its own logic and unfold itself to the listener without the assistance of a pre-arranged system. There is unlimited scope both in method and material, but all the more responsibility devolves upon the individual in achieving orderly presentation.

To return to technical considerations, this orderly presenta-

*In 'A Theory of Evolving Tonality', Harvard University Press, in which he presents the case that the next logical stage in the evolution of tonal organization would involve a new sub-division of the octave, twelve semitones forming the fundamental scale supplemented by its chromatic notes.

tion involves, against the background of an enlarged basic scale, new* inter-relations of melody and harmony, new methods of ordering progression and securing tonal coherence: in short, a fresh synthesis of the three elements of melody, rhythm, and harmony.

This being so, it might seem logical to examine the three elements separately, beginning with melody, which is the basis of music. But melody under these conditions is a broad and loose term. It can resolve itself into many types which emerge naturally in the historical study of actual music but which might seem no more than artificial distinctions in a purely abstract system of twelve-note possibilities. There would be the danger of putting the scale before the music and losing sight of the fact that the scale is really an abstraction, a classification of the sounds which have first been experienced. In certain fields of composition the twelve-note basis is obvious and all-pervasive. Bartok's exploratory mind has indicated some of the possibilities and illuminated them by his musical genius. The permutations are so large in number that a virtually unlimited field could be opened up in this way, by exploiting abstract potentialities. Mathematics, as it were, is waiting to be transformed into music. This, however, would not be a complete picture. National and personal modes of thought and expression have not been levelled into a musical Esperanto, so a purely twelve-note approach will not account for all of the musical experience of the twentieth century. The empirical continues to be the composer's way into the future and it takes its departure from some existing point in our experience. Rather than theorize from an abstract conception, then, it seems better to observe the growth of contemporary

*The fact that some of these new relationships may recall features which existed in music long before the present, or the classical periods, does not affect the main principle that a fresh synthesis has appeared in this century. Thus, although strands of parallel equal intervals have an ancient counterpart in organum, it is of little importance whether the latter-day use of the device is consciously derived from the earlier one. It is always probable that in a phase of re-orientation and experiment, many materials will come to hand which have been used before, some by chance, others by deliberate resuscitation, as in the case of modal melody. The point of the word 'new' is its relation to the last completely formulated system, the classical one as expounded in present-day academic theory.

methods out of the musical materials which have been already developed, to look at music in action and to allow it to throw light on the potentialities of the twelve-note scale. Our study of modern methods will therefore begin with two chapters concerning methods of progression characteristic of twentieth-century music. They will show why melody and harmony take particular forms, and reveal a logic which accounts for the inevitable use, and not merely the arbitrary choice, of the twelve-note scale. The three elements of the musical synthesis can then be reviewed, first singly and then in relation; and it will then be easier to see the tonal problems involved and what stage has been reached in solving them.

# CHAPTER SEVEN

# PARALLELISM

IN CLASSICAL PRACTICE every melody has a harmonic implication. In simplest form the melody uses the notes of a scale, and the chords which harmonize the melody are also made up of notes in that scale. The addition of decoration may disguise the obvious relation between melody and harmony and so too may temporary passage through other keys; but the essence of the system is that at all points a logical connexion can be perceived between the melody and the harmony, conceived together within a defined key. This synthesis of melody and harmony has been a distinguishing characteristic of Western composition for a thousand years, since the end of the period of organum. Emphasis has been laid now on the contrapuntal, now on the chordal elements, but there has always been some degree of interplay. The relations between chords within the key have been governed by established procedure, partly of root-relationship, partly of progression of parts designed to preserve the individuality of the component strands in a texture.

A different method of relating melody and harmony appears in Ex. 54, from *Minstrels* in Debussy's first book of Preludes. The notes of the chords depart from any major or minor scale to which the melody could belong, and the disposition of the chords is foreign to classical practice. There is one strand of melody reinforced by notes moving in parallel lines and free from any traditionally implied harmony. This parallel movement is the first harmonic feature so far discussed which cannot be related to classical tradition. It is not an enlargement or modification of former method, but a deliberate new departure. Its effect is not derived only from an 'unusual' juxtaposition of chords. Wagner developed the potency of that resource with-

out abandoning any principles of part-movement, and the
progression in Ex. 24, though showing juxtapositions independent of key, maintains contrapuntal independence in its
separately moving treble and bass.   The special characteristic

Ex. 54 DEBUSSY *Minstrels* from Preludes, Book 1

Music extract reprinted by permission of Durand & Cie

of complete parallelism is that an impression associated with a
harmonic group is sustained over a whole phrase by the exact
reproduction of that group at different pitches.   The attention
is focused on the harmonic quality of the group by its direct
impact on the senses, uncomplicated by any mental processes
which would be involved in the perception and inter-relation
of separate factors.   A definite musical logic is inherent for
instance in the quotation at Ex. 55 from Wagner's *Parsifal*:

Ex. 55 WAGNER *Parsifal*

'durch   Mit - leid   wis-send,   der   reine   Thor.'

the final E flat chord makes its effect in association with the
word 'fool' by evading the expected movement to a chord in
F major or D minor; and this effect depends on the listener's
assumption of a 'normal' thread of progression, and on his
assessment of the divergence from that norm.   By contrast

Ex. 54 (and earlier ones such as 36, 37*a*) show harmonies placed in contexts where contrasting groups do not present themselves for comparison; one chordal shape is singled out in order to make its effect purely as harmony. The recurring theme in the transitional stage was that of interest in the intrinsic quality of sounds. Parallelism lends itself to the exploiting of this interest by allowing harmony to be presented with the minimum of reference to its traditional tonal associations. It is one of the new methods not dependent on the chromatic decoration of a diatonic basis.

Among these chordal shapes, the triad still retains its fruitfulness and its capacity for fresh relationships. Even with traditional part-movement the effect of root-position chords having adjacent roots and modal colouring is most searching. The opening of Palestrina's *Stabat Mater* may be recalled (Ex. 56). The still more direct harmonic impact

Ex. 56 PALESTRINA *Stabat Mater*

made by completely parallel movement can be seen in Ex. 57. When allied to melody whose contours are firmly related to a tonal centre, parallelism produces no effect of tonal disruption. Ex. 57 shows phrases in which this melodic control is exercised. At *a*, *b*, and *c* a diatonic phrase is harmonized with different bass-treble intervals at each recurrence, causing various triads to be juxtaposed and to give their individual shading, but without disturbing the main tonal line. The same may be said of the Vaughan Williams example at *d*, as far as the end of the vocal phrase at A. In fact the prevailing effect is that of a single strand of modal melody except for the shimmer of harmony on the word 'praise'. Similar tonal continuity is evident at *e*, where a general parallel line of sevenths has

variously inflected constituent intervals, and so preserves a
diatonic character. This outlining of a melody suggests that
parallelism does not consistently have the effect of harmonic
emphasis. The apparent contradiction disappears if the device
is regarded as separating the elements of melody and harmony
from the complex of movement in which they were traditionally conceived together. In some contexts the harmony asserts
itself; in others, particularly in a quick tempo and with light

Ex. 57 . BARTOK  *Bluebeard's Castle*

Music extracts reprinted by arrangement with Universal Edition (London) Ltd.

texture, it is more likely that the shape and outline of the
melody will prevail and the parallel chords be regarded as
colouring of the melody, which takes on a glitter and a separate
distinctness instead of merging with a background.

Although parallelism can easily be associated with diatonic
melody its wider influence is felt when it is used to produce
progressions among the diverse chords of the twelve-note
scale. It then disrupts traditional tonal organization. The
fluidity which it thereby brings to harmony is to be observed
in the last two bars of Ex. 57*d*, where between A and B there
is a side-slip rather than a modulation to a strongly contrasted
tonal centre. The application of this resource for descriptive
purposes is natural; it was a common feature in the music of
the French Impressionist composers. Exx. 57*f* and *g* show
some of the parallel juxtapositions from Debussy's Prelude
*Ce qu'a vu le vent d'Ouest* (see also Ex. 11c), which are musically
sufficiently disjointed to allow the imagination to conjure up
correspondingly wayward physical images. Frequent use of
pedal-points in association with parallel strands bears witness

VAUGHAN WILLIAMS *Five Mystical Songs*, No. 5

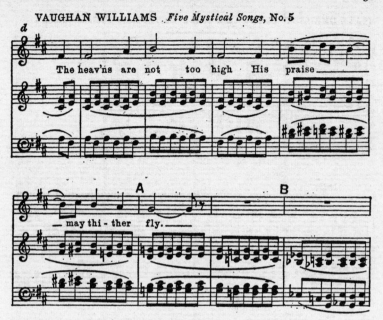

Music extract reprinted by permission of Stainer & Bell Ltd.

VAUGHAN WILLIAMS *London* Symphony, first movement

Music extract reprinted by permission of Stainer & Bell Ltd.

to their lack of tonal stability. (See Exx. 9 and 37*a* and the inverted pedal in Ex. 57*h*.) As diatonic contours, however, ceased to provide the ultimate standard of reference, it became easier to accept the full semitonal range of parallelism, to regard it as one of several normal methods of progression and dispense

(Ex.57) DEBUSSY *Ce qu'a vu le vent d'Ouest* from Preludes, Book I

Ibid

Music extracts reprinted by permission of Durand & Cie

BARTOK *Bluebeard's Castle*

Music extract reprinted by arrangement with
Universal Edition (London) Ltd.

with the adventitious aid of pedals or with suggestion of
special effects.

The traditional use of one or more composite strands within
a harmonic texture can be seen in the Beethoven extract at
Ex. 58, or in the richer part-weaving of the *Sanctus* in Bach's
B minor Mass. This resource takes on quite a new aspect, how-

Ex. 58  BEETHOVEN  Piano Sonata in D, Opus 28, fourth movement

ever, when the component intervals of a strand are exactly
maintained, instead of conforming to a diatonic chordal basis.
The internal structure of harmony becomes flexibly variable.
It may retain a triadic character, with modifications which are
really no more than new resources of colour; or it may lose its
chordal definition entirely and rely for its effect on the listener's
appreciation of separately moving lines. When a strand thus
proceeds by a regular succession of intervals, it provides a
method of giving order to sounds, and if the listener's mind is
open to perceive that order, to judge it in its own right and
not in relation to some presumed vertical blend, a wide extension of the field of harmony is made possible. At the same time
a correspondingly freer use of discord must be postulated.

In order to emphasize the difference between traditional
practice (as illustrated in the Beethoven example) and the
modern use of parallel intervals unrelated to a harmonic basis,
a quotation from the first movement of Bartok's second String
Quartet is given at Ex. 59. Subsequent examples can then
be more easily assessed in relation to the two extremes. Strands
consisting of parallel intervals are set in contrary motion at the
points *a*, *b* and *c*. The separate entries of the instruments,
based on a regular melodic pattern, are gathered together, and
their impetus is carried forward through these contrary motion
strands with a mounting harmonic tension at each repetition.
This is secured partly by the increased degree of discord in the
constituent intervals themselves (fourths and thirds at *a*,
predominantly minor sevenths at *b*, and major sevenths at
*c*), partly by the varied inter-relation of the strands themselves.   Interpreted in a traditional way the passage at *a*

*could* be related to a basis of chords decorated by retardations, but the spacing of the two upper parts in elevenths suggests

Ex.59 BARTOK  Second String Quartet, first movement

Music extracts reprinted by arrangement with Universal Edition (London) Ltd.

rather a preoccupation with the strand as a separate element, not as part of a chordal blend. The other two passages would defy such harmonic analysis. Their effect derives essentially from the movement of lines and the quality of intervals. It does not follow that vertical combinations are merely ignored or left to chance. The passage *a* leads to a seventh chord from which the second group of imitative entries emerges naturally, and *c* leads to a combination at figure 12 whose latent energy is released during several succeeding bars of development. A study of this movement reveals the greatest mastery of sonorous groupings and spacings, and an extraordinary range of degrees of tension.

Two more extracts from the same movement, at Ex. 60, will show the extent of this range, and at the same time will illustrate another common form of parallelism, in which one strand provides a complete accompaniment. The formula used at *a* can be applied with endless variation of detail, from the

Ex. 60  Ibid

simple triadic form as here to any of the numerous possible chordal shapes, or any strand of intervals. There is no need to multiply examples; several types have already appeared, such as the perfect fifth in Ex. 5, whole-tone chords, Ex. 13, augmented fifth, Ex. 51b, major sevenths in the last bar of Ex. 36c.

Apart from the intrinsic harmonic character of the accompanying strand, the musical value in such cases depends on the placing of the accompaniment in relation to the melody. The texture is that of two-part counterpoint in which one line is thickened or coloured. The principle of interplay of parts is therefore operative again, and with it the idea of varying degrees of tension. Ex. 60a illustrates this, in the momentary friction of simultaneous major and minor thirds; and 60b, in which the accompanying strand of augmented fourths is set against two melodic parts, shows the constant urge of Western music to interaction of contrapuntal lines leading to heightened points of discord (A), and subsequent relaxing (B), The particularly modern feature in this last example is that one of the contrapuntal lines is composite, and its constituent intervals are designed to be assertive and so avoid absorption into a chordal background. This became increasingly evident in the eight bars leading to this extract, where the strand began virtually as passing-note movement over a C sharp minor seventh chord and then acquired increasing independence as its intervals became major thirds and finally augmented fourths.

Between these extremes of chordal blend and assertive linear independence there is a wide harmonic field in which parallelism has a controlling influence. It was seen in Ex. 4 to preserve the continuity within one chord of a particular spacing, or at 32a of an appoggiatura group, or at 36 the shape of an elliptical decoration; and at Ex. 48 it was used to determine the actual chordal structure itself. The opening and closing bars of Debussy's La cathédrale engloutie show this structural influence, since the sustaining pedal is used to retain each successive group and build up a composite sound. Colouring of pedal harmonies, or background chords, in the manner of Ex. 61, which is the opening of Kodaly's Psalmus Hungaricus, may also be viewed as a structural function of parallelism, since the tremolando strand, avoiding a note-by-note decorative relation to a rigidly defined chord, provides a persistent renewal of the harmonic impulse.  The harmony is not static, but constantly recreates as it were its own tissues.

**Ex.61 KODALY** *Psalmus Hungaricus*

Music extract reprinted by arrangement with Universal Edition (London) Ltd.

It is this quality of freshness, this means of escape from the tyranny of an established chordal system, which gave such a vogue to parallelism in the first flush of modern harmonic expansion. Added to this musical value, it has a special technical utility as a method of organizing progression between chords. By maintaining the shape of a chordal group, it provides a recognizable order, independent of root or key relationship. It does not, in itself, ensure that this order has tonal continuity; it can only give coherence at the local points of progression, but provided it is used within a broad tonal framework it can be a most effective resource in associating together the equally available semitones of the twelve-note scale.

# CHAPTER EIGHT

# PATTERN

THE IDEA of pattern carries with it the implication of regularity of design produced by mechanical rather than imaginative means. It is certainly a method of securing order, though the artistic significance of such order might appear to be somewhat limited. It can, none the less, have more than a merely mechanical function, and it has played a part especially in formative and experimental periods throughout the development of European music.

Leaving out of account the element of pre-arranged pattern which is present in the basic material of music, i.e. in the set order of tones and semitones in modes and scales, the conscious use of pattern in the process of composition itself can be seen in the devices of canon, inversion, cancrizans movement, which were an indispensable element in the evolution of polyphonic technique and forms. Pattern serves a double function: it controls the general formal structure and contributes to the details of harmonic texture. In these two aspects pattern is an active force in later periods of technical transformation. The sixteenth century 'divisions' and variations rely upon a basic theme varied by figurative patterns as a means of extension and development; the prevalence of the ground bass in the seventeenth century bears witness to the same need for a structural prop. In both these forms, an apparently mechanical device eventually grew to full stature as a truly musical resource capable of rich development. They were both largely structural in function. Another kind of pattern, forming part of the harmonic detail itself, is the sequence, which is at home either in the balanced forms of the later eighteenth century, or in the continuously unfolding periods of Bach, or in the chromatic ranges explored by Liszt, Chopin and Wagner.

Up to this culminating point of Romantic harmony, the element of pattern inherent in the tone-semitone basis of the modes and scales had exerted its influence in directing progressions in relation to a tonic. In a scale formed entirely of equal intervals, whether whole-tone or semitone, this directing influence disappears. The need for some form of perceptible order asserts itself the more strongly if coherent relationship between the intervals is to be ensured. Our age has witnessed various approaches to this new problem of tonal organization, from the tightness of the Twelve-Note System of Schönberg through all variations of personal style to a complete empiricism at the other extreme. A common element in these diverse styles is the fact that harmony and melody are no longer restricted to shapes which can be referred to triad origins. Thus, in a simple form, the melody at Ex. 62*a* can be referred, by appoggiatura decoration, to a basic B flat

Ex. 62

triad, whereas that at *b* does not submit to any traditional analysis. It is a pattern of ascending fourths. It might alternatively be interpreted as the arpeggio of a chord built up in fourths, and in that case a harmonic basis of a new kind would be present. Context would decide whether the harmonic or the melodic element was predominant. In many contexts, however, such passages have clearly no chordal associations and they therefore represent a fresh aspect of the search for order in musical sounds.

Four general characteristics of twentieth-century music may well be borne in mind in this context. First, traditional tonal organization is not relevant when the tone-semitone orientation in its basis is abandoned. Secondly, the changed norm of consonance now permits a far greater number of sound-combinations, and pattern progressions are valid means for their production and organization. Thirdly, the spontaneous growth of harmony out of contrapuntal movement is an important present-day feature: pattern exercises its function in this very direction. Fourthly, harmony based on the triad and its close relationships within a tonal system has hitherto brought the mental and the emotional aspects of music into equilibrium. Whether or not it may be counted a defection from an ideal state of balance, a symptom of over-sophistication or of satiety with emotional states, there is a pronounced strain of intellectualism in art today and this can be seen in the exploitation of certain abstract features in the ordering of sounds. Both on technical and aesthetic grounds, then, there is today a suddenly enlarged scope for the use of pattern methods in securing fresh correlations of sounds.

Pattern in music is revealed in horizontal movement, i.e., in the relationships of sounds in succession. A regular succession of notes separated by the same interval is the most obvious melodic pattern; of this type, the chromatic scale (continuous semitones), and the diminished seventh arpeggio (continuous minor thirds) were common in traditional technique, whereas continuous whole-tones, major thirds, perfect or augmented fourths, did not find a natural place in classical harmony. Some illustrations of these regular series are given in Ex. 63. The passage at *a* has a chromatic scale in the upper part, and a complete succession of perfect fourths in the lower. It is virtually a traditional root-progression, with a new flavour added by the further element of pattern in the three-note groups of the right-hand part. The progression at *b* consists of a strand of sevenths ascending by semitones, combined with one of triads descending by the fixed interval of a minor third. This is pure pattern. Although there is nothing forbidding in the sounds of the vertical combinations, they are clearly not conceived as homogeneous vertical structures, and they owe their origin to the two separate chordal strands. At the same time, there is no bitonality, since neither strand can be said to have affinity with any particular tonic in this case; the device is one of colour only, and the pattern organizes apparently unrelated sounds to achieve this effect. Another harmonic feature, one of quite common occurrence, is seen in the same example. A diminished seventh arpeggio is formed by the successive minor thirds of the upper strand, but the diminished seventh chord never occurs vertically at any of the chordal combinations. The internal flavour of the harmony is quite different from that which would arise if the chords of the right hand strand were used as separate positions of one diminished seventh chord underlying the whole passage. Ex. 63c, based on stepwise movement in all parts, shows how the shape and texture of a passage may be largely suggested by pattern, but details are then consciously adapted to a desired musical end, in this case the particularly pointed discords at A and B. Tones and semitones are present neither in an unbroken pattern nor in a scale or mode, but adjusted to secure appropriate inter-relation of lines broadly conceived on a scalic design. Counter-point is bringing its influence to bear on harmonic groupings. There is justification for the use of what may appear to be mechanical procedures if they are fertilized by imagination.

The whole-tone scale, appearing as a regular pattern of intervals, may be associated with whole-tone harmonies (as for instance in Ex. 50c), in which case it is obvious that it merely represents a re-arrangement of notes of the same whole-tone chord. It was pointed out in Chapter Seven that strands of parallel intervals can form a pattern which affects to some extent the details of harmonic texture and of chord progression. On the other hand, the whole-tone scale may form part of a pure pattern movement, as in the left-hand part in Ex. 36c, where it is combined with a series of major third movements in the right hand and the resulting groups do not form whole-tone harmony. It may also be used as in the first violin part at Ex. 64, as a decorative addition to a pre-viously determined chordal basis with a bitonal flavour in this case.

Regular successions of minor thirds have been illustrated passim in Ex. 63, and major thirds in Exx. 25 and 36c. A feature worth noting in this connexion, and in that of the augmented fourth, is that they form a 'closed' series, which is repeated at every octave. Thus, a pattern repeats itself after

Ex. 63 RAVEL *Valses Nobles et Sentimentales*, No. 1

Music extract reprinted by permission of Durand & Cie

GOOSSENS 'The Gargoyle' from *Four Conceits*, Opus 20

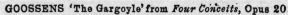

Music extract reprinted by permission of J. & W. Chester Ltd.

LENNOX BERKELEY *Etude*

Music extract reprinted by permission of Augener Ltd.

four minor thirds, three major thirds, two augmented fourths. This fact has a bearing on harmony if one of these series is combined with any other series, since new relationships are produced as the patterns get more (or less) out of step. Ex. 63b illustrates the point: the right-hand descending minor thirds, G E C sharp A sharp, repeat themselves an octave lower in the second bar with a distinctly added tang of discord against the left-hand groups. The point has musical relevance, for since the pattern gives rise to harmonic groupings which differ in the quality of their dissonance, cohesion, and spacing, it calls for taste and judgment on the composer's part. It underlines, moreover, the fact that harmony cannot be considered in the abstract, apart from the medium in which its sounds are presented. Strands of chords, or of intervals, if associated with different instrumental timbres, can be combined in ways which would be meaningless in a monochrome. This of course is no recent discovery; it has become part of all harmonic thinking during two centuries of orchestral evolution, but it has special significance whenever harmonic texture is being built up as the sum of separate linear strands.

A passage of augmented fourths (or diminished fifths), occurring in unbroken succession, has the effect of repeating an interval at different octaves rather than of producing an unfolding melodic series. Against the background of a defined tonality the indeterminate nature of the interval prevails, and consequently such a passage provides a simple modulatory device. An example occurs in the second movement of the Debussy quartet, where the interval D G sharp descends through three octaves and serves as a pivot, in the eight bars before figure 11, for the modulation which was shown in Ex. 27a. Debussy uses the same sequence of notes in *Pelléas*, at the end of Act III, Scene IV, to represent one of Golaud's moments of bewilderment and frustration. In the twelve-note scale on the other hand the augmented fourth does not have this marked effect of tonal disruption; it takes its place more as a normal interval without particular tonal significance.

There is no indeterminacy about a succession of perfect fourths. These fourths, and their complement the perfect fifths, have always formed part of the basic stuff of music, both melodically and harmonically, providing a framework which became clothed by the remaining intervals with increasing variety as harmonic experience developed. Today the prominence of these intervals suggests a parallel with 'functional' architecture, in which the structural lines emerge without adornment. The effect, even on the average contours of melody, has been revolutionary; it is all the more marked in instances which may be considered deliberately experimental. Ex. 65 gives a glimpse of such an approach in Schönberg's *Kammer Symphonie*, op. 9, with its rigorously maintained series of perfect fourths, at A cutting through the strands of whole-tone chords, at B combining contrary lines of fourths which settle, in the context after this example, into clearly defined six-part chords built up in fourths. More uncompromising in its dissonance against a chordal background is the ascending pattern of fourths at 2 in Ex. 102(a), from Stravinsky's *Sacre du Printemps*, where the composer might almost be using a painter's technique and applying raw colour for primitive effect, deliberately eschewing any blend. The absorption of successions of perfect fourths into the normal contours of melody, as opposed to bringing them into temporary high light, is seen in the next two

Ex. 64  BARTOK   First String Quartet, second movement

Music extract reprinted by arrangement with Universal Edition (London) Ltd.

examples. The ascending figure at *a* in Ex. 66 is one of the germinating motives of Vaughan Williams' F minor Symphony, and the phrase at *b* is the beginning of the melody of the second movement of Walton's Viola Concerto.

No useful purpose would be served by illustrating all the

remaining intervals, which are inversions of those discussed
above. From a harmonic point of view, the sixths and thirds
have close correspondence. Melodically sevenths have a far
more arresting character than their inversions the seconds,
and the frequent occurrence of major sevenths in modern
melody, as for instance in Ex. 88*b*, from Schönberg's *Pierrot
Lunaire*, is one of the technical manifestations of the expanded
range and tenseness of present-day music. (See also the sevenths
in the last line of Ex. 71*c*). Practical considerations of
compass make unbroken successions of these wider intervals
comparatively rare. Even the smaller ones already illustrated
are seldom used for more than a short stretch of their possible
theoretical continuation, and then as points of colour, as
cadenzas, or as modulating links, rather than as integral parts
of the musical thought and texture.

Ex. 65 SCHÖNBERG *Kammer Symphonie* Opus 9

Music extract reprinted by arrangement with Universal Edition A.G. Vienn/
(Alfred A. Kalmus, London)

There is far more flexibility of scope when pattern organization is given to short groups which through their variety of
contour can form part of the essential thematic material.

Ex. 66  VAUGHAN WILLIAMS  Fourth Symphony, first movement

WALTON  Viola Concerto, second movement

Music extracts reprinted by permission of the publishers, Oxford
. University Press

Some of these types can be classified and illustrated.  The
general trend of evolution underlying them all is away from the
secondary function of giving arrangement to notes within
already defined harmony, towards linear movements which
are independent of any chordal basis.

### Two-Note Groups

A group of two notes does not constitute a pattern; alone it is
no more than an interval.  Some element of repetition is needed
to show that the melodic character of that interval is being
maintained, and that its ordered pattern is contributing to
the musical organization.  Thus in Ex. 67a, the descending
scale of semitones is harmonized by alternate minor triads and
major ninths, brought into logical juxtaposition by the repeated two-note groups in the bass.  Each harmonic unit in

this case is a familiar chord.  At 67b the groups on the
second and fourth quavers are decorative links, which owe their
particular vertical constitution to the pattern in the bass.
The large part played by decoration was discussed in Chapters
IV and V; appoggiatura groupings, and empirical chords
produced by the movement of parts, are prominent features of
modern harmony, and the part-movements which control
these decorations often take the form of two-note patterns.
(See Exx. 33, and 37a).  Leaving the field of harmony in
which this reference to specific chords can be observed, two
further stages are shown in Exx. 68 and 69. In the first example,
the first chord of each successive pair has an appoggiatura
relationship to the second; a possible elliptical analysis of the
minim chords might be suggested, but the wider  context of the

Ex. 67  RAVEL 'La Pintade' from *Histoires Naturelles*

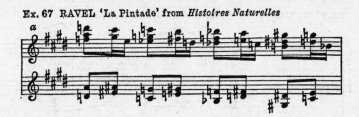

RAVEL 'Le Martin-Pêcheur' from *Histoires Naturelles*

Music extracts reprinted by permission of Durand & Cie.

movement shows the empirical nature of the combinations
and their derivation from a prevailing pattern.  In the Schönberg example, there is no question of harmonic blend.  The
piano and the orchestra contribute together to a composite

texture, with separate strands built up in clearly defined two-note groups. The break with any previous synthesis of melody and harmony is uncompromising.

Ex. 68 BARTOK Second String Quartet, second movement

Music extract reprinted by arrangement with Universal Edition (London) Ltd.

Ex. 69 SCHÖNBERG Piano Concerto, first movement

Music extract reprinted by permission of G. Schirmer Inc. New York
(Chappell & Co. Ltd. London)

Varying degrees of symmetry are present in these illustrations of two-note groups. At Ex. 67, the groups are separated by the same regular interval; at Ex. 69 there is no fixed order, but rather an insistence on the fifth-fourth and the seventh-fourth alternations. This singling out of a particular interval often serves to give coherence and sense of direction to melody, even if a strictly regular pattern is not continuously maintained. The extracts at Ex. 70a, from one of the complex melodic flights of Bartok's violin concerto, show perfect fourths, sometimes separated by a semitone, as at 1, or by a tone, at 2, or returning within their leap, at 3, but in each case imposing their character on the melody and guiding it firmly through ranges of notes which by traditional standards would seem to have no logical connexion. At b and c, the wider intervals, fifths and sixths, are given prominence.

**Ex. 70  BARTOK  Violin Concerto, first movement**

Music extracts reprinted by permission of Boosey & Hawkes, Ltd.

In the twelve-note scale, individual intervals exert a greater influence on melody than is possible within the narrower boundaries of the diatonic scales. If the listener can eliminate from his mind all normally expected contours arising from a convention of harmonies, and if the composer can give adequate point to his thematic material, there is no reason why true twelve-note melody should not germinate entirely from that initial material and carry within itself its own logic. A quotation at some length from the second movement of Bartok's Second String Quartet is given (Ex. 71), to illustrate this kind of flexible development and to show the place which pattern devices can take in a typical twelve-semitone texture. The basic figure consists of a semitone and a leap, which is foreshadowed in the brief introduction *a*, but which makes its strongest impact in the move from minor to major third shown at *b*. Some of the subsequent transformations of this

Ex. 71 BARTOK Second String Quartet, second movement

Music extracts reprinted by arrangement with Universal Edition (London) Ltd.

Music extracts reprinted by arrangement with Universal Edition (London) Ltd.

Music extracts reprinted by arrangement with Universal Edition (London) Ltd.

Music extracts reprinted by arrangement with Universal Edition (London) Ltd.

Music extracts reprinted by arrangement with Universal Edition (London) Ltd.

figure can be seen in the longer quotation at *c*, where fragments of chordal harmony are also present (as in the augmented
fifth chords at A, the triads at B, and the more novel groups at
D); but the musical and technical preoccupation is largely with
the germinating figure. Its influence is clear not only on the
character of the melody, but also in the vertical results which
follow from contrapuntal combinations in pattern form, at C
and E. It is a special feature of Bartok's style, most marked in
his middle period, that an attitude of intellectual curiosity
about the potentialities of musical materials can exist along
with what is commonly regarded as an instinctive or intuitive
approach to composition. Devices of pattern may seem to lean
heavily in this intellectual direction, but if they can be shown to
contribute to works of musical vitality they have a valid
contribution to make to musical development.

The flexible play with the characteristic intervals of a
melody, which is one of Bartok's individual traits, recalls
Bach's treatment of the subject of the A major Fugue, number

Ex. 72 · J. S. BACH  Fugue in A from *The Well-tempered Clavier*, Book 1

19 of the '48', and the comparison serves to emphasize the function of the pattern treatment in the modern work. Ex. 72 shows thematic character being determined by a prevailing perfect fourth interval, and the kind of modification which that interval may receive. The subject *a*, has one of its fourths augmented at *b* to appear in minor form, and at *c*, the stride of all the intervals is widened, but in all three cases in conformity with the scale convention within which Bach naturally worked. The Bartok examples have the same musical purpose, *i.e.* the development of thematic material in varied aspects; but they have to create their own ordered relations from point to point against a background of twelve equal semitones instead of a scale of seven notes with already ordered relations.

### Groups of Three and More Notes

The number of possible combinations of intervals rapidly increases as larger groups are considered. They can all be brought within the sphere of music in the twelve-note scale, since there is no predestined order to which melody must conform. Some of the types are shown below, with little comment, since the underlying principles are the same as those of two-note groups.

Three-note patterns from varied contexts can be seen in Ex. 73, as also in earlier examples at 29*a* and 63*a*.

At *a* triad shapes are retained, but at *b*, which is continued as an ostinato for five bars against an independent violin part, there is no harmony in the chordal sense, but an arrangement of tone-colours as a background to melody. 69*c* is a regular three-note melodic pattern, and *d* combines an ostinato of five notes in the right hand with a three-note group in the left.

The four-note groups in Ex. 74 preserve a regular symmetry. At *a* the double strand of seconds, moving by semitone steps, accounts for the internal constitution of the harmony over a pedal; at *b* the first-inversion triads succeed one another at the regular interval of a major third, again over a pedal.

New flavour is extracted at Ex. 75*a* from old triad materials, by the five-note groupings combined with the interval shapes in the left hand; at *b* the old principle of decorative figuration over an established bass is present, but with emphasis on the wedge-shaped six-note pattern rather than on the constituent notes of a chord. It is only a step from there to the use of melodic ostinato alone as the background of melody, one of the most common modern resources in accompaniment, either in strict pattern form, or with various degrees of flexibility.

### Contrary Motion Pattern

The simultaneous sounding of a melody and its own inversion, which has been called 'reflection' or 'mirroring', is a pattern device which like all the others can operate within a defined harmonic scheme or can imply a complete negation of the traditional view of harmony. The second movement of Beethoven's Piano Sonata, Op. 90, contains an example of the first type (Ex. 76). A very different quality of harmony emerges in the next two examples (77*a* and *b*), where the texture has no centrally conceived harmonic core. In the first case the emphasis is melodic, with a scherzando treatment of the contrary lines, widely separated both in tone-colour and in pitch, which makes for easy acceptance of features of harmonic novelty. In the second case, the two outer strands produce a

Ex. 73  DEBUSSY  *Pelléas et Mélisande*

Music extract reprinted by permission of Durand & Cie.

SCHÖNBERG  *Pierrot Lunaire*

Piano
Flute
Clar.

Music extracts reprinted by arrangement with Universal Edition A.G. Vienna
(Alfred A. Kalmus, London)

BARTOK  *Mikrokosmos* No. 128

Music extract reprinted by permission of Boosey & Hawkes Ltd.

form of harmony and a bitonal accompaniment to an inner
melody; they have a descriptive purpose (the title of the piece is
*Night*), supplying a framework of extensive space, and their
separative tendencies reinforce the suggestion of space and
emptiness.

Ex. 74 RAVEL 'Le Cygne' from *Histoires Naturelles*

Music extract reprinted by permission of Durand & Cie.

VAUGHAN WILLIAMS *London* Symphony, first movement

Music extract reprinted by permission of Stainer & Bell Ltd.

Ex. 75 LENNOX BERKELEY *Etude*

Music extract reprinted by permission of Augener Ltd.

BARTOK  Sixth String Quartet, first movement

Music extract reprinted by permission of Boosey & Hawkes Ltd.

## Wider Structural Aspects

In nearly all cases, the examples of pattern treatment which have been given have occurred in textures which also include other harmonic features.   Regular melodic designs have a valuable function in controlling progression at given points, but they involve too much sacrifice of the qualities of variety, elusiveness, suggestion, which are essentials in art, if they are maintained with any obviousness over long periods.   They can however contribute unobtrusively to the basic structure of whole movements, as the ground-bass did in the past.   In

Ex. 76 BEETHOVEN  Piano Sonata in E, Opus 90, second movement

Examples 78*a*, *b*, and *c*, for instance, the control of progression owes much to basic patterns which do not obtrude themselves, but which do account for the particular successions of harmony. In the first case they are short, in the second they underlie an extended section; and in the third they persist amid varying textures throughout a whole movement, in which the pattern

Ex. 77 SHOSTAKOVICH Sixth Symphony, second movement

Music extract reprinted by permission of Boosey & Hawkes Ltd.

BRITTEN 'Night' from *Holiday Diary*

Music extract reprinted by permission of Boosey & Hawkes Ltd.

shown in brackets in the bass is maintained in passacaglia fashion, but mounting by successive semitone steps at each reappearance.

At this stage we pass beyond the range of harmonic analysis to that of structure in general, and so beyond the scope of this

Ex. 78 DEBUSSY *Jardins sous la pluie*

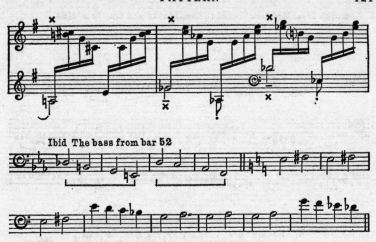

Ibid The bass from bar 52

Music extracts reprinted by permission of Durand & Cie

ROY HARRIS  Third Symphony

Muted Strings

D.B.

This kind of texture is maintained for 178 bars; the juxtaposition of the chords is governed by the pattern shown here in the Double Bass part.

The value of these notes

moves from tied semibreves to semibreves and finally minims

Music extracts reprinted by permission of G. Schirmer Inc. New York
(Chappell & Co. Ltd London)

RAWSTHORNE  First Piano Concerto, second movement (*Chaconne*)

*Andante con moto* ♪ = 76

Music extract reprinted by permission of the publishers, Oxford
University Press

study; but the reference to some extended applications of
pattern serves to complete the survey of the potentialities of
the device, and to illustrate once again the fact that both the
point-to-point progressions and their broader organization in
whole sections now owe more to melodic or contrapuntal
movement than at any time in the past.

# CHAPTER NINE

# MELODY

THE LAST two chapters have been concerned with new methods of movement and have shown that completely new musical textures can be produced without resorting to chordal innovation. Less emphasis has been laid on new chords as such than on new relationships between familiar materials; but vertical structure itself has been seen to undergo considerable transformation, merely as a by-product of horizontal movement. To maintain a true perspective in the study of harmony, the nature and function of these horizontal movements must be borne in mind and their effect on melodic contours observed. Examples 71 and 72 pointed to the fundamental difference in this respect between the classical and the modern methods, that is, between music written within an established convention and music which has to convey its own order and significance without the help of a pre-existing system. To some extent, new flavour in music can be obtained by applying new resources of harmony to traditional melody, even of a familiar diatonic type. In most cases, however, new character is deeply imprinted in melody itself. This may broadly resemble the shapes of earlier music, but its details have important new implications. The purpose of the present review of melody is to examine such new features and their function in contributing to new textures and methods of progression.

The simplest form of divergence from the classical method of organization arises from the use of modal melody. The nationalist movements brought into music as a cultivated art far more than a merely superficial return to folk-song and to modal idioms. They fostered new centres and styles of creative activity, which drew in varying degree upon the main European stream, but derived their motive force from their own native manners of thought and turns of expression. Thus there are, in addition to the basic differences between national traditions, numerous shadings in melody which result from varied degrees of absorption of resources from the main stream.

Let us take first a few examples of modal melodies which contain features new not in themselves but in their manner of presentation (Ex. 79). We shall then see that the traditional relations between harmony and melody are here changed in a significant way. This is not a result of any new shape or colour in the individual chords, or even of their non-classical manner of progression, but rather of allowing long stretches of melody to unfold without change in the accompanying harmony. Modal melody, in its original form as plainsong or folk-song, was independent of any accompaniment at all; its contours were merely related to a clearly defined tonal centre. When melodies came to be combined and their resulting vertical combinations had become familiar as chordal harmony, each complete melody was felt as a total of many smaller elements conditioned by harmonic and rhythmic impulses of a basically regular kind. The rate of chord change, or 'harmonic rhythm', was a factor of paramount importance in classical harmony. Nationalist composers focused attention again on melody in its own right, with freedom from necessarily regular metre and from point-to-point harmonic implications. In so doing they both broke away from classical convention and cleared a way for much constructive development. The principle is seen at work in Ex. 79 where in each case the melody is presented purely as a single line, no longer related in Wagner's sense as the 'surface of harmony' to its accompanying background. The latter is infinitely variable in possible shape and detail, from pedal-points, single and multiple, plain and ornamented, to chord-structures of any degree of complexity, and from simple undulatory movements to elaborate ostinatos of either melodic or rhythmic character. The illustrations given in Ex. 79 are simple and limited in extent. They serve however to call attention to this immensely fruitful resource of presenting melody, which is complete in its own tonal organization,

independently of any harmony which would control its contours or dictate its progression. This represents the simplest
form of musical texture based on a tonal centre. Change from
one centre to another takes the place of modulation in the

**Ex. 79 VAUGHAN WILLIAMS** *Benedicite*

Music extract reprinted by permission of the publishers, Oxford
University Press

**KODALY** *Marosszeki Dances*

Ibid.

Music extracts reprinted by arrangement with Universal Edition (London) Ltd.

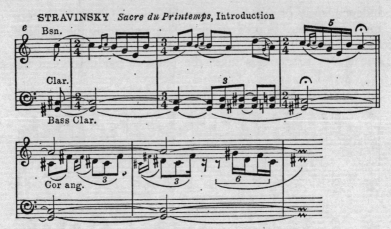

STRAVINSKY *Sacre du Printemps*, Introduction

Music extract reprinted by permission of Boosey & Hawkes, Ltd.

classical system, an obvious example occurring at the double-
bar in 79*a*. Used for wider structural purposes, groupings of
these centres can provide the tonal framework for whole movements; the first movement of Vaughan William's fifth symphony provides a clear-cut example.

In these extreme instances the sense of harmonic progression
is at a minimum; but there are many intermediate stages of
interplay between melody and harmony before traditional
modal contours are finally obscured and completely twelve-
note melody is reached. The influence of harmony in bringing
extraneous semitones into play is easy to observe in Ex. 80,
where triads are juxtaposed in regular whole-tone steps, at A,
and so pass beyond the diatonic bounds of the mode. The
notes of the melody at B are not merely chromatic additions to
an 'orthodox' mode; they have become an essential part of an
extended basic scale. It will be recalled that some scales of
the Magyar type include as basic elements semitones additional
to those of the European diatonic modes, and so exert an
influence even apart from harmony. This is felt not only in
new turns of phrase, which sound exotic to Western ears, but
more fundamentally through their absorption by Bartok into his
own composite melodic idiom, completely independent of class-

ical tonality. Ex. 81 illustrates the double influence: the C sharp
in bar 5 of *a* is a normal scale note, and thus takes a natural
place in the phrase; Bartok's own fluid use of supplementary

Ex. 80 ·VAUGHAN WILLIAMS *London* Symphony, second movement

Music extract reprinted by permission of Stainer & Bell Ltd.

Ex. 81 BARTOK *Mikrokosmos* No.98

Music extracts reprinted by permission of Boosey & Hawkes Ltd.

semitones appears in the two phrases at *b* and *c*. The whole
piece, an unaccompanied melody of twenty-eight bars, has a
clearly defined tonality; although it touches all the semitones of
the twelve-note scale. It indicates the function which melody,
organized in recognizable phrase-shape, can exercise in co-
ordinating these semitones.

The next examples, from Bartok's *Divertimento for String
Orchestra*, 1939, illustrate in brief the general transition from
modal to twelve-note melody.

At 82*a*, the opening of a twelve-bar melody is shown. which is essentially in the Dorian mode, with F as its tonic, The notes E natural and B natural, marked X at their first

**Ex. 82  BARTOK** Divertimento for String Orchestra, first movement

Music extracts reprinted by permission of Boosey & Hawkes Ltd.

appearances, are decorative. They suggest the idea that melodic phrases can be firmly based upon certain pivotal notes and other semitones be given a subsidiary place within their contours. Here the main framework of the melody is supplied by the basic mode; in completely twelve-note melody there can be entirely free choice of the pivotal notes.*

The relation of the accompanying harmony to the melody is interesting. It is based, like the melody, on a tonal centre F, but it does not share the Dorian character of the melody. In the first bar, for example, it strongly asserts two notes, A natural and B natural, in a way which openly contradicts the mode; and throughout, subsidiary colourings and momentary frictions are produced by the choice of discordant relations with the melody. There is a mild compromise between dissonant counterpoint and pedal harmony, and the controlling influence is not any basic chordal progression but a forthright melody organized over its whole course on a broadly modal basis.

The quotation at *b* shows new features arising in the subsequent development, the melody now containing certain pattern elements which allow it to progress freely among the twelve semitones without reference to a mode. At 1, the successive fourths produce a new phrase-shape; at 2, a modulation or change of centre is effected by the major third groups; and at 3, the pattern allows complete contrapuntal independence to be secured against the merest nucleus of harmony.

These examples suggest the general line of development in the neo-modal sphere, one parallel to that already discussed in transition from the classical key-system. As the modal or scale basis is obscured, devices for achieving order and direction in horizontal movement acquire increased importance, and the national and traditional streams merge in the international one of composite melody.

The international stream of music includes a vast complex

---

*If any smaller interval than a semitone enters into the practical field of music, one of its natural functions could be some such decorative one. The third of Szymanowski's *Mythes*, Op. 30, for violin and piano, opens with such an auxiliary note undulating a quarter-tone below D.

I

of styles and historical traditions and many contrasting types of melody. Whether these are of the 'unending' Wagnerian variety or of the more fragmentary nature familiar in Debussy or Stravinsky, they will not be discussed here except from a limited technical point of view: how, in the absence of a defining basic scale, are they in fact organised? Contours clearly derived from associated harmony are not included in this limited inquiry, although it is well to remember that the scope of melody has been continuously widened as a result of harmonic expansion, and the way thereby prepared for new melodic shapes.

Free and equal use of the semitones of the twelve-note scale is postulated in this particular inquiry. There are two main systems designed to bring these semitones under ordered control, one Hindemith's and the other Schönberg's. In the first, harmonic factors have an important place and control is exercised by planned chordal progression, not by empirical horizontal movements. Successions of melodic intervals, both between the roots of chords and on the surface of the harmony, enter nevertheless very largely into this planning; and it is not possible to assess the influence of one element in the system without examining the whole.

### The Hindemith System

Hindemith bases his system on a twelve-note scale derived from the harmonic series, and indicates the relationship of these notes to a generating tonic in the order shown in Ex. 83*a*, which he calls Series 1.

Series 1

Ex. 83
*a*

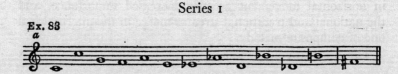

The closeness of relation diminishes from left to right. A second series, 79*b*, determined by the differential sounds of the respective intervals, shows the relations between the scale notes themselves:

Series 2

⟫⟶ indicates the root of the interval.

Harmonic strength and value is greatest in the intervals on the left, and least on the right; conversely, melodic tendency is greatest between intervals on the right and diminishes to the left.

On the basis of these relationships the structure and the progression of chords is regulated. Greatest harmonic stability is possessed by those containing the strong harmonic intervals, and tension increases as intervals of less harmonic value predominate. The root of the 'best' harmonic interval in a chord is considered to be the root of the chord, and the relationship between roots is assessed by examining the intervals formed between successive roots. Thus in a succession of chords with roots C D B flat A G C, the perfect fourth, G to C, is the best harmonic interval, and its root C asserts the strongest claim to be considered the tonic, or tonal centre, of the whole phrase. This claim is strengthened by the double appearance of the note C. The issue would be complicated by the appearance in a phrase of rival intervals of equal strength, but a properly planned context would ensure the predominance of the desired tonic. In this respect, horizontal movement has a vital influence on the organization of tonality, securing it in each separate context by adjustment of the melodic intervals between roots and not by reference to chords with a fixed harmonic function.

Hindemith proceeds to the separate study of principles of melodic structure, and his Series 2 is called upon once more. He is careful to stress potential harmonic implications of a melody. Starting from the obvious case of successive leaps which form the arpeggio of a triad, he goes on to examine the implicit chordal suggestions present when prominently placed intervals are filled in with intervening decoration. Rise and fall of tension secured by the placing of melodic intervals is discussed in detail. Hindemith makes no claim to any systematic relation of the points of melodic climax to those which he closely controls in the harmonic field, but he points to the obvious desirability of seeking, in practice, as close a correspondence as possible.

From this summary, two points emerge which are pertinent to our present examination of melodic influences on texture: one concerns the control of root progressions, the other the harmonic implications of melody. In both cases there is a movement away from a rigid conception of chordal harmony based on diatonic foundations, towards one which seeks to correlate twelve-note melodic lines both in their vertical and their horizontal aspects. Yet in principle the system rests on the same foundations as the classical system. It is broadened to permit a truly functional use of every semitone and every chordal combination; but in organization of tonality by root progressions, in recognition of relative harmonic tension and repose, and in the interplay which it postulates between melody and harmony, it continues the general development of harmonic method since the seventeenth century. When he emphasizes true melodic character as opposed to the outlining of harmonic blocks, Hindemith touches the Achilles' heel of any harmonic system; but his own provides no automatic safeguard against harmonic commonplace. That is in the last resort the responsibility of the composer himself, who can now achieve a trite effect with an arpeggio of fourths just as well as his predecessors could with an arpeggio of thirds.

## The Twelve-Note System

The Twelve-Note System of Schönberg has no affinity with the technical methods of the past and would seem to have no place in a study of harmonic evolution. But though it represents a new departure, it does face the central problem of twentieth-century music—the tonal organization of twelve undifferentiated semitones—and its contribution is therefore of vital interest in any technical inquiry.

Its essential features have often been described. Briefly, it cuts the Gordian knot of the tonal problem and organizes the twelve semitones not in relation to a central tonic but in a pre-determined order which varies with each composition. The term 'atonal', which has been applied to such music, is literally accurate, as it indicates the absence of a controlling tonic; but it does less than justice to a synthesis expressly designed to achieve coherence among its constituent tones. The twelve semitones in their predetermined order are called a 'note-row' or series, which may be used also in retrograde motion, in inverted form, or with the inversion in retrograde motion. Transposition to any pitch is an available resource, so that with four forms of the series and twelve different semitone positions for each there is a choice of forty-eight variants of the initial series. In order that no individual note may attain prominence, and thereby any semblance of a tonic function, repetition of notes (except as a subsidiary rhythmic feature) is avoided; the series is normally presented as a complete entity, constantly recurring as a whole but with varying redistributions of its semitonal components. This varying distribution is secured by the fact that the notes of the series may either follow one another melodically or two or more may be combined harmonically.

Ex. 84 shows three aspects of the system. At *a*, which is the opening of the Fourth String Quartet, Op. 37, of Schönberg, the whole series is played by the first violin from bars 1 to 6. It is also continuously present through the depth of the texture, as will be seen by reference to the numbers placed beside each note. It appears four times in these given bars, each three-note section of the melody being accompanied by the remaining nine notes of the series in rigid numerical order.

At *b* (bars 25 to 27 of the quartet), contrapuntal treatment is seen. The original form of the series is divided in the first bar between second violin and viola; the inverted form of the series starting on G is used in the next bar; and in the third bar, the original form of the series appears in the two upper parts simultaneously with the inverted form in the two lower parts.

Ex. 84 SCHÖNBERG  Fourth String Quartet, Opus 37

Considerable variety in the manipulation of detail is maintained throughout the work, but one more example will illustrate a point of considerable significance.  Bars 229 to 232 are shown at 84c to draw attention to the shapes, both melodic and harmonic, which are given to the texture without departing

Music extracts reprinted by permission of G. Schirmer Inc. New York
(Chappell & Co. Ltd. London)

from the principles of the Twelve-Note System. (The inverted
form of the series starting on C sharp, then on C natural, is
used up to the second beat of bar 230; the original form, on A
flat, starts on the second beat of bar 230 in the viola.) Here, in
contrast to the strictly successive order of the notes of the series
in Exx. *a* and *b*, there is a selective approach, particular intervals
being brought into prominence in the several parts of the texture. The series makes its continual reappearance in the groups
marked A B C D E F, its twelve notes in each case sounding so
nearly simultaneously that the impression of the original order
comes near to being effaced and new pattern arrangements are
allowed to assert themselves.

Two relevant conclusions may be drawn from this short
review of features of the Twelve-Note System. The first is the
exclusion of any previously accepted idea of tonality and the
substitution of a kind of cellular organization which pervades
the texture and gives it homogeneity. The second is that the
motive principle determining the character of these cells is
melodic and not harmonic. This is true both in a general and
in a detailed sense. In a general way, the structure throughout
is conditioned by a melodic factor, the series. In a detailed
way, shape is given to each individual portion of the thematic
material, as in Ex. 84*c*, by adjustments made within the
original framework of the series. Here there is a common
ground between Schönberg's system and musical tradition.
In the latter, choice of interval is comparatively unfettered,
whether in the horizontal direction or in organizing the vertical
groups. In the Twelve-Note System also, particular choices
can be made, but they are compensated by limiting factors in
the horizontal progression or in the accompanying vertical
texture, since movement is not free until all the notes of the
series have been heard. These limitations are accepted for the
purpose of securing homogeneity. In the classical system limitation existed too, in the nature of the diatonic scale and the
principles of chord progression. The tendency was constantly to
absorb new findings and reduce the limitations, with the result
that the original system of tonal control progressively lost its
definition. Schönberg's system, on the other hand, is designed

from the beginning to cope with complexity, since the twelve
semitones form an entity, not a group of separate elements each
to be related to a centre.

One of the ways of obtaining thematic definition was seen in
Ex. 84c under the closely limiting conditions of the Twelve-
Note System. It remains to observe ways of seeking thematic
and tonal definition under the freer conditions of music which
owes allegiance neither to the traditional key-system nor to the
more abstract system initiated by Schönberg. Pattern enters to
some extent into any such method of securing order in the melodic
sphere. The underlying principle is that of selecting particular
intervals and allowing their character to have free play without reference to basic scale or controlling harmony. Regular
successions were illustrated in Chapter Eight. The extracts at
Ex. 85 show that thematic character can be imparted by a
prevailing interval without the need of mechanical repetition
in series form. The first example, with its prevalent thirds,
strongly tends to outline normal triad harmony, though the
juxtapositions from bars 8 to 13 would not be normal by
classical standards. In the second example the tenor melody has
a clear-cut organization which is independent of chordal
harmony. It emphasizes seconds, both major and minor. In
these close stepwise movements it illustrates incidentally the
tendency of twentieth-century harmony to close compression,
in contrast to the general evolution which is towards widening
range. The zig-zag figure in bars 3 to 5, formed of interlocking

Ex. 85 RAWSTHORNE Symphonic Studies.

Music extract reprinted by permission of the publishers, Oxford
University Press

whole tones, is a Bartok finger-print, one which carries with it a
strong assertion of melodic independence.  The restatement of
the first bar phrase in inverted form at bar two should be

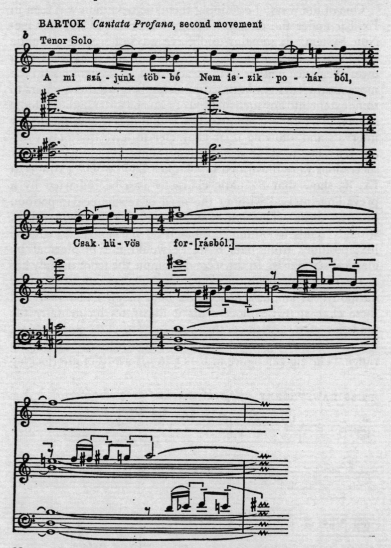

BARTOK  *Cantata Profana,* second movement

A mi szá - junk töb - bé   Nem is - zik  po - hár  ból,

Csak  hü - vös   for-[rásból.]

Music extract reprinted by arrangement with Universal Edition (London) Ltd.

noticed. The device of inversion takes a more natural place in
the twelve-note environment, where all steps up or down are
equal, than in the diatonic, where they are varied.   In this

RAWSTHORNE, **Symphonic Studies**

Music extract reprinted by permission of the publishers, Oxford
University Press

example only a short phrase is involved. It happens that the longer melody of 85a is used in exact inversion (at figure 51 of the movement) and application of the resource over still longer periods is not uncommon, either with a certain degree of flexibility, as in Bartok's Fifth String Quartet, or with complete strictness as in the case of Hindemith's *Ludus Tonalis*, where the three complete sections of the Introduction are repeated in inversion and retrograde motion at the end of the work. The third example, 85c, bears the impress of the interval of a seventh, often in the composite form of a fifth plus a third (a), or a third plus a fifth (b), or with other variants (c, d) in the internal filling-in of the total interval. The accompanying parts are also quoted, to give the flavour of the harmony. The general contours would suggest a classical B minor, with a central modulation to D; but the detail of the texture is attributable neither to scale, mode, nor chordal harmony but derives from the interval shapes of the melody.

Given such independence of any fixed scale degrees, there is scope for considerable variation in the restatement and development of themes. Ex. 86 illustrates this flexibility. The theme which is first presented as at *a* recurs in the form shown at *b* with adjustment of some intervals in bars 3 and 4. (The transposition given at *c* makes the modification readily

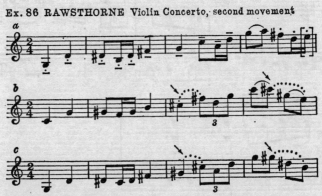

Ex. 86 RAWSTHORNE Violin Concerto, second movement

Music extracts reprinted by permission of the publishers,
Oxford University Press

apparent.) This suggests a comparison with chromaticism and modulation as in the classical system. Strictly speaking, neither of these terms is relevant in the absence of any defined key; but in practice it is clear that salient notes can be brought into prominence and establish a tonal centre, as the G centre for instance at 86*a*. It is then a matter of choice whether the composer wishes to use semitones liberally or sparsely within his general framework, and to modify intervals and inflexions either for structural or for expressive purposes. The principle is the same as the classical one, once a general tonal orientation has been established: chromaticism (colouring of a plain basis), and modulation (change of tonal centre), are aspects of the same tradition which varies only in the details of its interpretation.

Similarly there is continuity of principle in the use of sequences, germinal motives, and obviously recognizable phrase-shapes like the wedge pattern at Ex. 87. (The subject of the *Wedge* Fugue in E minor for organ by J. S. Bach may be recalled.)

**Ex. 87 BARTÓK Fourteen Bagatelles, Opus 6, No. 2**

Music extract reprinted by permission of Zenemükiadó Vállalat, Budapest

There is moreover much melody which, as far as constituent intervals are concerned, has a great deal in common with melody of all ages. In such cases the imprint of a particular period is due to other than purely melodic factors, as will appear in the discussion of rhythmic and harmonic features. (See particularly Ex. 91.)

This brief digression to observe some of the technical points of contact between modern and traditional melody serves to emphasize, by contrast, the one important respect in which twelve-note melody has its own character and can exert a controlling influence on texture. That is, in its choice of specific intervals to govern and colour each stage of progression. In this way it is independent of pre-established scale or harmony, and its real achievement is that of providing new forms of order in the horizontal direction. It is perhaps this conscious cultivation of intervals and their colours, as well as the desire for increased tension and range, that leads to the frequent use of octave transpositions, as in the intervals of Ex. 88.

Ex. 88 STRAVINSKY *Sacre du Printemps*

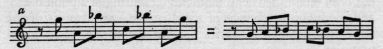

Music extract reprinted by permission of Boosey & Hawkes Ltd.

SCHÖNBERG *Pierrot Lunaire*

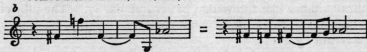

Music extract reprinted by arrangement with Universal Edition A.G. Vienna
(Alfred A. Kalmus, London)

In these contexts, the sevenths and the ninths, although only substitutes for seconds as far as their letter names are concerned, have a far more intense effect as musical sounds in the widened forms of the intervals.

In contrast with this search for new effect in a positive way, there may be something of a negative attitude, an avoidance of old formulae, in many cadenza-like fioritura passages, as at Ex. 89, where the alternate tone and semi-tone construction of the running passages gives a 'touch of novelty' to what is a familiar outline.

Finally we should bear in mind that the twelve-note scale is not constantly called upon in full in twentieth-century music. There is plenty of melody which follows diatonic contours, perhaps often with new relation to the rest of the texture, or with fresh disposition of the melody (à la Britten), in relation to the tonic of the scale. Ex. 90, with its Phrygian flavour within

Ex. 89 RAWSTHORNE Symphonic Studies

Music extract reprinted by permission of the publishers,
Oxford University Press

Ex. 90 BRITTEN *Spring* Symphony, Part 1, *The Morning Star*

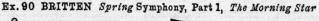

Music extract reprinted by permission of Boosey & Hawkes Ltd.

F major, indicates the method. There is also a great field of
melody which itself is influenced by new harmonic considerations, but that is not within the scope of this chapter, which is
concerned with melody as an active force in determining the
detail of texture and progression.

# CHAPTER TEN

# RHYTHM

RHYTHM (that is, the grouping of notes according to their duration in time), may be examined as a separate element which can exist without affecting the character of the simultaneous sounds which we call harmony. That purely separate aspect of rhythm lies outside the present scope; it belongs to the wider spheres of composition and observation of modern manners of thought. Thus when Stravinsky, in the coda of *Les Noces*, makes a rhythmical transformation which distils the essence from the previous thematic material of the work, he is using the element of rhythm for a structural and dramatic purpose.

Although much rhythmic experiment and innovation can take place in this way without direct effect on the constitution of harmonic groupings, it does produce textures which are markedly different from those normal in classical music. The contrast is shown in Ex. 91 where the same melodic contour can be seen in classical, pre-classical, and post-classical form. At *a*, the melodic fragment appears on the 'surface of harmony' and in a clear-cut metrical framework, with an unmistakable harmonic rhythm and a placing of the melodic climax in relation to a regularly recurring metrical accent. In the Byrd example at *b* there are no such regular strong points of harmony and metre embracing all the elements of the texture.

Ex. 91 BEETHOVEN Piano Sonata, Opus 110, first movement

Music extract reprinted by permission of Boosey & Hawkes Ltd.

The melodic shape and rhythm are maintained in the several voices (though with subtle variation at bar 3 in the change from ♩. ♪ to ♩ ♪), and a vertical blending of consonant intervals persists. Any attempt to impose a regular metrical order would obviously make nonsense of the verbal rhythms. To

K

pass to the third example (c), over intervening centuries in which the metrical view first developed and then lost its predominance, is to renew acquaintance with melody of rhythmic fluidity, expanded in length and possessing non-diatonic contours, but closer in spirit to Byrd than to Beethoven. Apart from any new characteristics in the vertical combinations, we have here a texture which does not lend itself to analysis in the classical manner; and the difference is due to the changed rhythmical approach. The normal expectations in the timing of chord-changes in that system, the relation of horizontal lines to harmony at regular intervals of time, the clearer definition and more symmetrical placing of cadences, all correspond to the patterns of regular verse metres, and all tend to give way to the rhythms of free verse or of prose.

The transition was not sudden. It had already advanced far in the long-drawn melodies and sparse cadences of Wagner by the time of *Tristan* (completed in 1859), and it was bound up with natural development in the harmonic field, such as freer use of decoration. Besides these internal developments and natural growths, fresh rhythmic influences came into the main stream from folk-song and dance, from Oriental and African sources, from the admission of primitive material for musical treatment, from jazz, as well as from conscious experiment in new rhythmic schemes. In so far as those influences affect rhythm alone, there is no point in quoting examples; but inasmuch as these influences have an effect on musical texture, some adjustment in habits of listening is involved. The effect may be independent of the vertical structure of harmony and its influence may be exercised rather in the same subtle way as that of tone-colour, producing variations of emphasis, perspective, light and shade. These are important matters in themselves, and it is necessary in analysis to trace the effects to their source. Rhythm, as a separate element, is one of these sources.

There are further respects in which innovations in rhythm do affect the constitution of harmonic groupings, and these can be more specifically illustrated. Some of them involve the pattern principle. A simple case occurs (Ex. 92a), in the cadenza

Ex. 92 LAMBERT Concerto for Piano and 9 Players

Music extracts reprinted by permission of the publishers, Oxford
University Press

of Constant Lambert's *Concerto for Pianoforte and Nine Players*.
A contrary-motion melodic pattern is present, and at the same
time the exact points of synchronization are determined by the
rhythmic pattern of five quavers in the right hand against three
crotchets in the left. The example at *b* is more complex.
The texture consists of three strands, the lowest having a
regular pattern both in melody and rhythm, the middle one
being almost regular, and the upper apparently irregular in
rhythm but having subtle internal subdivisions. The direct
effect of these rhythmic combinations on harmonic groupings

is here unmistakable. Fresh vertical groups are being produced throughout, and the contrasts are especially noticeable
if one point is selected, *e.g.* the F natural at the beginning of
the three-note figures in the middle part, and the harmonies
observed at its successive repetitions, marked*.

In Ex. 93, instead of a combination of varied rhythmic
patterns, a non-metrical melody is placed against a regular
ostinato, with the obvious effect of reversing the harmonic
combination of melody and accompaniment, as for instance
at A and B. Judged in isolation, the vertical groups at those
two points have different harmonic flavours, though in the
musical context the harmonic quality is subordinate to the
general rhythmical effect. This is true of many passages which

Ex. 93 STRAVINSKY *L'Histoire du Soldat*, Part I

Music extract reprinted by permission of J. & W. Chester Ltd.

avoid symmetrical character either by non-regular successions in
time, or by the simultaneous use of differing rhythmical schemes.
It may be that such rhythmic patterns emerge more clearly
to the eye of the score-reader than to the ear of the listener.
They are sometimes picked out in different tone-colours; but
whether clearly perceived or not, they have the effect of cutting
across the old customary metrical divisions with which harmony
was associated, and producing new vertical groupings of an
empirical kind and often of secondary importance in the
musical context.

# CHAPTER ELEVEN

# REGULAR CHORD STRUCTURES

## I

### IN THIRDS, SECONDS, SIXTHS, AND SEVENTHS

THE PRESENT century has seen a movement away from any exclusively chordal conception of musical texture. Nevertheless there remains a large amount of music which is chordal, and the aim of the following chapter is to seek whatever forms of order can be found in its methods of vertical structure.

It must be said at once that there is no contemporary system of harmony which is valid for all composers. No doubt such a thought has always struck students of the creative work of their own day. Common elements are more easily to be observed when time has given perspective to the view. Yet there exists today an unprecedented situation, in that no norm of reference is recognized in the combining of simultaneous sounds. The dividing line between consonance and dissonance has become blurred or non-existent, and composers claim the right to the free use of any vertical groupings. As far as acoustic considerations enter into practical musical composition, the upper partials of the harmonic series are regarded as available in chord-structure without exception or limitation. This view is taken by Alois Haba, who in his *Neue Harmonielehre* (Leipzig 1927) even includes the partials beyond the sixteenth, which are smaller than a semitone. Without trying to find acoustic sanction for the procedures of composers, we must start from the position that any group of notes, even one which would include all the twelve semitones, is available in chord-structure. The fact is witnessed by a large number of works written before 1914, and it derives authority not from any system but from the practice of composers whose work bears the stamp of genius and integrity. Musical theorists have accepted this authority in the past, and they have no logical reason for condemning the adoption of the full range of semitones in chord-building.

In a period of such obvious experiment and rapid expansion of resources, it seems reasonable to expect an increased consciousness of technical method among composers. Yet, apart from the personal systems of Hindemith and Schönberg, there is little evidence available outside the music itself; and new technical features have to be sought in a complex of old and new, from which few self-evident principles can be deduced. Some works reveal a conscious interest in particular devices, and so provide specific clues for the theorist; but much of the new flavour of harmony arises less from the radical alteration of method than from extension of old practices. Throughout the development of classical technique we may observe a constant accession of discord and an increasing subtlety and variety of simultaneous sound-groupings. Although the triad basis of that harmony cannot be questioned, the triad shape itself became disguised by decoration. A dividing line might be drawn, in theory, between those harmonies which can and those which cannot be analysed as thirds-structures, but in practice many of these groupings are indistinguishable to the ear. It is not surprising therefore that methods involving empirical choice of vertical intervals and their groupings should replace a system in which the actual sounds heard are theoretically related to a simpler generating basis.*

In view of these general considerations, any classification of chord-structures must be arbitrary, neither complete nor authoritative. Some definite and regular methods can be illustrated; for the rest, little more than suggested interpretations of individual contexts can be offered. The fluidity of technique so often mentioned in this study forbids any dogmatic approach.

*In this connexion it is interesting to observe that Schönberg, in his *Harmonielehre*, expressly denies the existence of 'unessential' notes, as also does Haba in his system.

## Chords Built in Thirds

Before proceeding to new intervals in chord-structure let us first examine some unfamiliar aspects of vertical building in thirds.

There is an obvious extension of traditional practice in the free use, without resolution, of seventh, ninth, eleventh, and thirteenth chords, with or without chromatic inflexion. This is a matter of degree rather than of principle; it was referred to in the study of transition. In itself, it serves to move the harmonic centre of gravity further into the realm of discord, and to disrupt tonal relations as previously conceived.

If the matter of inflexion is pursued further, on the lines of Ex. 94, the fact emerges that structures in thirds tend to split into subsections. The first two possibilities, showing all the thirds minor at *a* and all major at *b*, are familiar, the first producing the diminished seventh chord, the second the augmented triad. Enharmonic change is assumed at 1 for practical purposes, and so these intervals produce a closed

Ex. 94

series which repeats itself at each octave. At *c* and *e* the series built up of alternate major and minor thirds makes use of all the twelve semitones before it finally repeats itself. From the sixth note upwards at *c*, tonal relationship with the root tends strongly to disappear, and new separate tonal implications are set up by the sub-sections, such as the various triads indicated by brackets at *c*, or the seventh-groups at *d*. Bitonal or polytonal suggestions are apparent at once. Here there is a distinctively modern chord structure which can be derived from the traditional method of building in thirds. Theoretically, the possibility was always present. Historically,

Ex. 95 BARTOK   Fourteen Bagatelles, Opus 6, No. 2

Music extract reprinted by permission of Zenemükiadó Vállalat,
Budapest

BARTOK   Violin Concerto, first movement

Music extract reprinted by permission of Boosey & Hawkes Ltd.

Music extract reprinted by permission of Boosey & Hawkes Ltd.

it could not arise before chromatic notes came to be accepted as not merely decorative but integral members of the whole chord. A stronger norm of dissonance, too, must be accepted and textures consisting of composite strands rather than of whole chords traversed by single horizontal lines. The principle is seen at work in Ex. 95, which illustrates some of the regular alternations postulated in Ex. 94. The chords are in broken form, perhaps conveying a sense of melodic pattern more than of chordal harmony; but they reveal Bartok's concern with the potentialities of vertical structure. The quotation at *b* from the same composer's Violin Concerto shows the emergence of a bitonal chord (bar 233), by the addition of thirds below and above the initial G sharp of bar 228. The chord is then reproduced as a harmonic unit at different pitches (bars 239, 241). No sense of different keys is present here. Contrast the combination seen in Ex. 95*c* with its conflicting C major and minor tonalities in the violin parts, and the dominant seventh of A flat supplied in addition by the trumpets. (Another instance of complete bitonality in the vertical structure itself, from Stravinsky's *Sacre du Printemps*, can be seen at Ex. 102*a*).

A further departure from the traditional practice of building in thirds is illustrated in Ex. 96. Its special feature is the placing of a note, or notes, to secure discord, a principle which will be discussed separately, apart from regular chord-structure itself. It is mentioned here in connexion with building in thirds because a number of modern chordal groupings have a

Ex. 96 SCHÖNBERG *Das Buch der hängenden Gärten*, No. 13

ending

Music extracts reprinted by arrangement with Universal Edition A.G. Vienna
(Alfred A. Kalmus, London)

deceptive appearance of being constructed in the classical manner, *i.e.*, rising from a root, whereas a more natural analysis assumes the placing of sounds in their individual relations to one another.

This discordant placing is obvious at *a*, where the opening and closing chords of the accompaniment are given. At *b*, a steady friction of dissonance is maintained both by the prevailing major sevenths, or diminished octaves, in the broken-chord groups themselves, and in the inter-relation of these smaller groups within the whole texture. These discordant intervals, formerly reserved for the tensest harmonic moments, appear regularly in Schönberg's music of this period. Whatever type of structure he may be using, this degree of friction is likely to be present.

Another principle which applies to all types of chord may well be mentioned here in connexion with composite structures in thirds. It is that of tone-colour. If multiple groupings like those in Ex. 94 are used, gradation of discord can be regulated by the spacing and pitch of the sub-sections, and by orchestration. A stereoscopic effect can be produced, and subordinate groups which have a certain coherence and blend can be set against other groups of different colour, quality, and strength, so tempering the hard impact of the superimposed thirds. The idea of multiple strands in the texture is again prominent. In fact, if chord-structure involves multiple groups with strong internal frictions, it cannot be studied purely in the abstract. The medium used and the disposition of the chord in the context must be taken into account, and these factors form a necessary part of the act of composition. Tone-colour can in fact be regarded as a separate resource available to the composer, apart from harmony, with which it was formerly associated. It then becomes a subject for separate study. Within the field of harmony its influence is to be felt in all the types still to be discussed. It is a positive factor both facilitating 'awkward' combinations and placing in unexpected new lights a merely static harmony. It also imposes limitations, particularly in choral music, where something of the true character of vocal tone is sacrificed when astringent groupings are used.

### Structure in Seconds, Sixths, and Sevenths

The use of notes in groups of seconds was mentioned at the outset of this study as a device popular in the early years of the century for securing new chordal shapes and new colour effects. (See pp. 20 et sqq.) The principle, at that stage of harmony, was one of adding notes to a pre-existing chord, producing a blurring of outlines.

In the famous 'sheep' variation (No. 2) in Strauss's *Don Quixote*, added notes appear in a different light. Three-note clusters of semitones are presented against a basic D major chord in the strings; but spaced as they are and picked out by their orchestration, they do not form part of a total chordal blend, but emerge as separate entities. The purpose is descriptive in this case, and these groups could hardly be analysed as chord-structures. They are onomatopoeic rather than harmonic, colouristic rather than structural. Yet, as so often in the evolution of harmony, resources first used for colour and expression pass into the general currency of musical language, to be used sometimes unconsciously and sometimes as a deliberate experiment. The stage is then reached at which seconds in themselves can provide the whole harmonic texture, as regular structures in compressed form.

Bartok's fourth quartet shows the potentialities of the second, both melodically and harmonically. The whole work could be quoted as an example of musical logic based upon certain technical premises, the inter-relations of seconds, major and minor, providing most of the matter for discussion

Ex. 97 BARTOK Fourth String Quartet

*a*    second movement

*b*    third movement

until the last movement, where the perfect fifth comes into the foreground. Some of the details of treatment are seen in Ex. 97. The first two examples are diatonic. In each case a seven-part chord is built up; at *b* the middle note of the group is absent in the chordal background, but it is supplied when the cello enters

with the melody.   Ex. 93c shows a regular semitone group formed, at X and Y, as each instrument enters and sustains its note; and at Z the entries are rearranged to form a chord of four whole-tones.   In the final glissandos, it may not be too fanciful to observe, apart from a heightening of tension, a still greater compression of intervals, melodic steps being dissolved away entirely into a progression of imperceptible gradations.   The process at d is a reversal of the one used at b and c; here, the melodic entries, instead of moving outwards from a single note, converge with mounting tension upon the final semitone group.   A last example, at e, from another work by the same composer, shows progressions between whole-tone groups of seconds in the right hand of the piano part, the first in parallel and the second in contrary motion.

Such examples show Bartok investigating the possibilities of harmonic grouping among the smaller intervals organized in regular form.   There remain the larger intervals of the sixth and the seventh.   Chords built up exclusively of these intervals do not appear as regular features of harmony.   The wide intervals, reproduced upwards throughout the texture, make

(Ex. 97)

*d* . second movement

Music extract reprinted by arrangement with Universal Edition (London) Ltd.

*e* BARTOK Second Violin Sonata

Music extract reprinted by arrangement
with Universal Edition (London) Ltd.

for unwieldiness and considerably reduced harmonic cohesion. Sporadic groupings do occur, as for instance the sevenths at Ex. 99*f*, which have the appearance of being regular structures; but far commoner are textures in which these intervals contribute their influence as separate strands and sub-groups. The last chord of Ex. 96*b* illustrates this use of sevenths, and Ex. 97*f* that of sixths. The latter example brings the wheel

WALTON Violin Concerto, first movement

Music extract reprinted by permission of the publishers, Oxford
University Press

full circle, for here it is once more the triad which provides the basis of the harmony. The parallel with structures in thirds is very close. In fact, if the thirds in Ex. 94 are replaced by their inversions the sixths, exactly the same harmonic results will be observed, with the reservation mentioned above about unpractical spacing. A new issue however is raised by the question of inversion, which will be discussed in connexion with non-regular chord-structure.

# CHAPTER TWELVE

# REGULAR CHORD STRUCTURES

## II

### IN FOURTHS AND FIFTHS

INTEREST IN the sound of fourths and fifths, which has been evident in much of this century's music, has prompted experiment in building chords entirely of these intervals. Signs of curiosity about such chord-formations began to appear in the late nineteenth century. Gerald Abraham, in *A Hundred years of Music*, refers to early examples of the fourth-chord, for instance in Scriabin's Op. 2, No. 3 (1886), Satie's *Le Fils des Etoiles* (1891), Borodin's E Flat Symphony (begun in 1862), and in Schönberg's *Pelléas et Mélisande* (1902). Technical development, as usual followed a gradual course, keeping fairly close to traditional practice in the early stages. Thus, Exx. 94 *a* and *b*, from Debussy's orchestral *Nocturnes*, 1900, show the fourth-chord shape, adopted for its colour, yet having a fairly close appoggiatura relationship to basic triad harmony. Schönberg, in using fourth-chords, seems to have been at first preoccupied with their relation to traditional harmony. In his *Harmonielehre*, for instance, he gives resolutions to triad harmony. The appearances of this chord in his *Pelléas*, referred to by Professor Abraham, are shown at Ex. 98c. They resolve in this case; the first to a minor triad, the second to an augmented triad. Again, the opening of the same composer's *Kammer Symphonie* (1906), given at 98d, shows an appoggiatura interpretation of the opening fourth-chord, in its resolution by stages to the F major chord in the fourth bar.

There is however no mistaking the full adoption of this

Ex. 98 DEBUSSY 'Sirènes' from *Nocturnes*

Music extracts reprinted by permission of

M. Jean Jobert

SCHÖNBERG *Pelléas et Mélisande*

SCHÖNBERG *Kammer Symphonie* Opus 9

L

(Ex. 98)

Music extracts reprinted by arrangement with Universal Edition A.G.Vienna
(Alfred A. Kalmus, London)

BARTOK  Violin Concerto, first movement

Music extract reprinted by permission of Boosey & Hawkes Ltd.

kind of structure in its own right (Ex. 98*e*), at a later point in
the *Kammer Symphonie*.    The beginning of this section was
shown in Ex. 65.   The chord appears here in broken and
unbroken form, in six parts and in five, and is moved
bodily as a strand of parallel intervals.    It takes its place in
the *Kammer Symphonie* both as a device of colour and as an
element in the thematic and harmonic structure.    With the
same dual function it has become current harmonic practice
among composers of widely divergent styles.    It is worth

pausing to look at some of its purely technical characteristics,
Ex. 99*a* shows it in completely regular form, in three, four.
five, and six parts, and the series could be continued to form a
complete twelve-note chord, using all the twelve semitones if
perfect fourths are maintained throughout. Alternatively, varied
inflexions are available, as in Scriabin's *mystic chord* at 99*b*,
or the series could be completely diatonic, as at *c*.   Multiple
chords containing many different notes have been used, but in
average textures smaller units from the whole chord are
generally selected.   Thus *d* omits one central note from a
regular structure in perfect fourths, and *e* omits two from the
diatonic series.   It is possible that at *f* Schönberg is either
selecting in this way from a complete fourth-chord with varied
inflexions, or else building in sevenths.

The notes of the chord at 99*e* are shown at *g* with closer
spacing,   and *h* shows  other  readily  manageable  spacings

Music extracts reprinted by permission of G. Schirmer
Inc. New York (Chappell & Co. Ltd. London)

derived from the complete chord.   The suggestion of sub-
groups in the texture appears again, and of a more empirical
approach to the use of the fourth-chord.   A single three-note

**Ex. 100 MOERAN** Violin Concerto, second movement

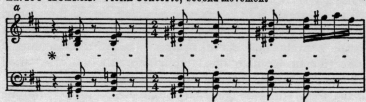

**SCHÖNBERG** *Das Buch der Hängenden Gärten*, No. 6

Music extract reprinted by arrangement with Universal Edition A.G. Vienna
(Alfred A. Kalmus London)

**BARTOK** Second Violin Sonata

Music extract reprinted by arrangement with Universal Edition (London) Ltd.

group can give the characteristic colour of the fourth interva
to a composite structure, as Ex. 100 will show. The three
quotations there show a gradation of discord from the mild
groups at *a*, through *b* with its sharply inflected sevenths,
to the bitonal texture at *c*.

Some of the general characteristics of the fourth-chord have
now been examined. We have seen it used as a complete
chord-structure in itself and as an added device of colour.
Used as a unit of basic harmony, it raises the question of chord-
progression, and of the fourth-chord's relation to surrounding
harmony. It presents no difficulty when linked to other
harmonies by decoration or part-movement, as in Ex. 98*a*,
*b*, *c*, *d*, but at 98*e*, the last phrase, marked 1, shows that
successive positions of the same fourth-chord are no more than
movements up an arpeggio; there is no real chord change. The
first two bars of the same example contain some element of
variety, since the higher notes of the chord, appearing in bar 2,
differ strongly from the lower ones, quitted in bar 1. Yet the
change is one of colour, not of root. This is similar to the
effect of the continuous use of one whole-tone chord or scale.
It was seen above, in Chapter Two, that semitone movement
from the one whole-tone series to the other was necessary to
secure a feeling of harmonic movement; and in the same way,
movement can be secured by moving from one fourth-chord to
another built on any one of the four semitones lying on each
side of its own bass. This is seen in the semitone movement
from bar 2 to 3 and in the middle of bar 4. It is more strongly

Ex. 101 BARTOK  Second String Quartet, third movement

marked when contrary motion is present also, as at $f$; and that example shows a complete use of fourth harmony and melody, strongly directed to its tonal objective, *i.e.*, the entry of the solo violin on B.

Control of the contrapuntal lines of the texture then seems to be particularly necessary when these chords are used. In themselves they cannot be said to possess a root.* Any note of the fourth-structure may be selected as a centre, and fourth intervals balanced on each side of it, and if given sufficient prominence in the context, that note can acquire a certain tonal stability. Bartok's method of addressing himself to this problem is illustrated in No. 131 of his *Mikrokosmos*, where the note E flat emerges clearly as the tonal centre of the piece, with fourth-structures balanced above and below it.

(Ex.101) SCHÖNBERG Piano Concerto

Music extract reprinted by permission of G. Schirmer Inc. New York (Chappell & Co. Ltd London)

---

*Examination of the fourth-chord from the acoustical point of view shows its significant difference from the traditional triad of thirds. The upper partials and the resultant tones produced by the respective chords are:

Upper partials:

Generating chord:

Resultants:

Two points emerge: each three-note group (shown in open notes on the bass stave), has its own character emphasized by the partials above it, thirds at *a*, fourths at *b*, fifths at *c*; and whereas at *a* and *c* there is a strong focusing of the resultant tones on the bass note C as a root, there is a considerable vagueness in the case of *b*, the fourth-chord.

The fourth-chord, like any basic harmony, can be decorated. Ex. 101*a* shows an example from Bartok's Second String Quartet.

Some flexibility in spacing may be seen at Ex. 101*b, c, d*, but

(Ex.101) VAUGHAN WILLIAMS *London* Symphony, second movement

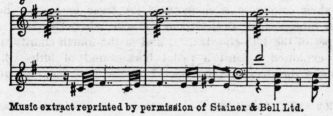

Music extract reprinted by permission of Stainer & Bell Ltd.

BARTOK Second String Quartet, third movement

Music extract reprinted by arrangement
with Universal Edition (London) Ltd.

it will be noticed that the true identity of the fourth-chord is preserved in each of these cases. Thus at *b*, the right-hand group of harmonics obviously represents a respacing of a four-part fourth-chord to lie easily under the hand. At *c*, the upper tremolando group does not necessarily in itself imply derivation from a fourth-chord, but as in the previous example, the clear definition is provided in the bass (bar 3). Ex. *d* has an open spacing of a fourth-chord which was heard in close position in the previous context. Inversion of the notes of a fourth-chord, *e.g.*

where its own identity becomes more obscure and other intervals are introduced, raises issues which will be discussed in Chapter Thirteen.

### Chords Built in Fifths

These chords, like those built in fourths, can be used either for their colour or as elements of the basic harmony. Both these functions are illustrated in Ex. 102a, where the particular shapes of the fifth-chords at 1, and of the fourth-chords at 2, are exploited against a pedal background of fifths which supplies the structural framework of the harmony. At 102b

Ex. 102 STRAVINSKY 'Danses des Adolescentes' from *Sacre du Printemps*

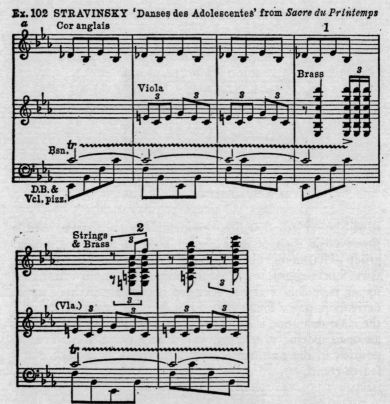

Music extract reprinted by permission of Bossey & Hawkes Ltd.

Music extract reprinted by permission of Boosey & Hawkes Ltd.

the two types of chord occur simultaneously and provide a cadential combination in which the orchestral scoring underlines the separate nature of the groups, four flutes playing the upper chord, and four oboes playing the lower, built in fifths.

The fifth-chords at 102c are employed structurally, supplying the complete harmony, instead of being subordinate groups in a composite texture. Full chordal use of fifths in this way is considerably rarer than that of fourth-chords. Apart from a certain unwieldiness and loss of harmonic cohesion which increases with the widening of the constituent intervals of a chord, there is a special assertiveness in the character of the fifth interval itself which militates against a chordal blend, except in association with the third as in a triad. It may be considered that a chord built in fifths conveys a strong impression of being a structure of thirds, with alternate notes omitted; it has too, like that traditional structure, a strong acoustical reinforcement of its lowest note as a root. (See the footnote on

page 166.) The parallel with structure in thirds is further underlined in Ex. 102a, where latent bitonal possibilities emerge clearly in the central C chord played by the violas.

Vertical grouping in fifths seems to be used less for the production of block chords than for the influence of the fifth intervals themselves as part of a composite structure. The fifths may contribute to the spacing of the chord, as in the

Music extracts reprinted by permission of J. & W. Chester Ltd.

BARTOK Fourth String Quartet, second movement

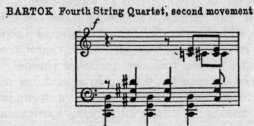

Music extract reprinted by arrangement with Universal Edition (London) Ltd.

cases of the last chord of Bartok's First String Quartet (Ex. 53d and the ninth-chords of Ex. 102d). Or they may be designed to give colour to a strand of intervals, as in the violin part of Ex. 93 or the upper stave of Ex. 102e. The bitonal placing of the two strands in the viola and cello at Ex. 102f further emphasizes this separation. Any inflexion of the perfect fifths, as seen in the last group at Ex. 102e, softens the hard edge of the intervals, producing in this case a complete

MILHAUD First String Quartet, last movement

Music extract reprinted by permission of Durand & Cie.

merging of the strand into a total chord. A final example, 102g, is added, showing how the use of the fifth-chord as a vehicle for tone-colour, already strongly evident at Exx. 102a and b, is carried to the extreme point where organized harmonic thought gives way to a purely physical presentation of the tone of the open strings of the instruments.

# CHAPTER THIRTEEN

# NON-REGULAR CHORD STRUCTURE

## I

### NEUTRAL CHORDS

BOUND UP with the system of harmony based on triads is the principle of inversion. The theory was formulated in 1722 by Jean Philippe Rameau, though the chord-shapes which he was later to describe as inversions had long been familiar in practice, at least as early as in fourteen-century fauxbourdon.

Has this principle of inversion any relevance to the newer chord forms reviewed in the last two chapters? A doubt is raised at once by the duplication of the group marked X in Ex. 103*a* and *b*. The one at *a* is derived by inverting a fourth-chord, the one at *b* by inverting a fifth-chord. Moreover, the fourth-chord itself may appear as an inversion of a fifth-chord, as seen in the first and last groups at *b*, and in fact it will be found that every possible inversion and respacing of the one chord can be equally well derived from the other. Two examples are shown at 103*c*. If chords are to be classified and named, there is something defective in a method of analysis which attributes different origins and names to one and the same group.

The anomaly does not end with the simple case of the fourth- and fifth-chords. Ex. 104 shows some of the chord-shapes which result from inversion and respacing of four-part chords

Ex. 103

Ex. 104

built in diatonic seconds (or equally well from their inversions the diatonic sevenths).   In fact, every group thus derived from a second- or seventh-chord differs from every product of a fourth- or fifth-chord, and the difference is accentuated if either whole-tones or semitones are used in building the second-chords.  It might seem therefore that the basic distinction be-tween these family groups is still preserved and that the principle of inversion has value here in facilitating the recogni-tion of these differences of character.

Inversion however ceases to have meaning when chords of six or more different notes are used.  Ex. 105 shows five chords which use the same six notes, and in theory each could be

Ex. 105

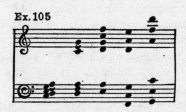

described as an inversion of any of the others.  But to the ear each of these groups has a completely individual character, which is changed if the arrangement of its constituent intervals is altered.

Repeated reference has been made throughout this study to the empirical choice of intervals for their colour and character.  This seems to be an obvious extension of traditional practice* and of nineteenth-century processes tending to obscure

*In the case of the triad itself, resonance and character vary considerably with the spacing, and with the interval formed between treble and bass. Cf.

the basic triad in its simple form. But although this gradual evolution has made the question of inversion seem academic, a radical difference does appear between classical and modern harmony, and it is a difference of kind, not of degree. In the former system, every group of notes was open to analysis, which reduced it to simple terms and disclosed its function in each individual context. In twentieth-century harmony there emerges the idea of groupings which are completely empirical, both in their individual structure and in their relation to one another. We may divide these structures into two main categories, differing from each other in degree of dissonance.

As was seen in dealing with chord-structure in general, the dividing line between consonance and dissonance has become blurred or non-existent. The word discord can in fact no longer bear the precise meaning which it had in classical harmony. In that system it had an absolute, not a relative value; it was 'not-concord'. If a standard chord, the triad, no longer exists as a norm, there can now only be relative discord, or different degrees of tension. In twentieth-century music it can be affirmed that there is a broad differentiation between the more acutely dissonant intervals, the minor seconds and ninths and the major sevenths on the one hand, and the milder major seconds and ninths and minor sevenths on the other. The latter class has attained as it were a position of neutrality between the strongest dissonances and those groups (the triad and the classical consonant intervals) which still remain absolute concords.

For the sake of clarity, the non-regular chords in which the neutral intervals prevail will be described here as Neutral Chords, to distinguish them from the concords and from the more strongly dissonant groups.

## Neutral Chords

The type of chord referred to under this heading has already been illustrated more than once in passing. (See Exx. 42, 53 and the pedal chord in 79c.) More extended examples of the use of such chords are given in Ex. 107, in order to reveal their general harmonic character, particularly the absence of clear-cut lines and vivid colours.

Although these chords are meaningless apart from their context and without their appropriate spacings, Ex. 106 may serve to show the basic features of their structure, and their place in the graduated scale of dissonance. At *a*, a systematic method is adopted in the construction of three-note chordal shapes, which are shown in close spacing. Of all possible three-note combinations within the octave, those shown in black notes belong either to traditional triads or seventh-chords, whole-tone chords, chords built regularly in seconds or fourths, or those which contain minor seconds or major sevenths.

Ex. 106

There remain the four groups shown at *b*, which are strictly within the definition proposed for neutral chords. This is a purely grammatical procedure, and it is not suggested that any such isolation occurs in musical composition. It serves, however, to bring these groups into perspective against the background of other harmonic resources.

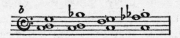

In contrast to classical harmony, the seconds and sevenths have become absorbed as stable elements in the chord itself, and need no resolution. Compared with groups containing the sharper dissonances, on the other hand, the neutral chords have a negligible feeling of friction. (Contrast the chords of *b* when their inflexions are changed to those at *c*; or, without

resorting to such an artificial extreme, see the quotations at Ex.
107*b* and *c*.) Some of the most characteristic four-note groupings are given at Ex. 106*d*, and five-note ones at *e*, again with
omission of the most obvious overlappings with traditional and
whole-tone harmonies.

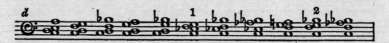

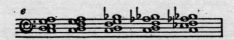

So much for the component notes of the chords. Spacing,
pitch, and tone-colour play a large part in their musical use,
but their relation to the general body of harmony remains as
indicated in Ex. 106. Thus, the 'pale, still water' chords of
Ex. 53*c*, reduced to simplest terms, are:

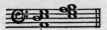

and this level of harmonic intensity may be compared with that
seen at Ex. 57*h* from the same work.

The austerity of Stravinsky's neo-classic harmony as compared with that of his early ballets is at once apparent in the
first quotation at Ex. 107. Against the harp ostinato of the first
bar, neutral chords, together with an occasional diatonic
seventh, provide the harmony until the last two bars. At X,
a sharper point is given, partly through the scoring for wind,
and partly through the semitonal placing of the two trombones
in the bass. The spacing and the progression of the neutral
chords is here largely controlled by a strand of parallel sevenths
and fourths. This quotation is typical of a large amount of
quiet-toned harmony. An even level is maintained in this

calm introductory passage, but interplay with other types of harmony can produce a virtually unlimited variety.    Exx. 107*b* and *c* show respectively an increase and relaxing of

Ex.107 STRAVINSKY *Orpheus*, First Scene

Music extract reprinted by permission of Boosey & Hawkes Ltd.

WALTON  Viola Concerto, second movement

Music extract reprinted by permission of the publishers, Oxford University Press

M

Music extract reprinted by arrangement with Universal
Edition A.G. Vienna (Alfred A. Kalmus London)

tension in the progressions from 1 to 2. The first is virtually a traditional root-progression from a B chord to a seventh-chord on F; the second arises directly from a parallel progression within the texture.

Through this adaptability to old and new associations the neutral chords mix easily in the most varied harmonic environments; and in thus widely establishing themselves they have considerably affected the norm of consonance. All the neutral chords contain a major second; and in so far as this interval comes to be regarded as consonant, an old landmark is being replaced by a new one, since for nine centuries of Western music the third has been regarded as the smallest consonant interval. The Western ear is being attuned to ever smaller intervals in harmonic combination. But although seconds have become tolerable concords, they have not been incorporated, as were the thirds, as the basis of any regular system of harmony, and the same applies to any composite structure of which they form a part.

The neutral chords, then, have not a specific technical function, but they do fulfil some general purposes in ordinary usage. They occupy a position midway between greater discord and completely accepted concord. In the setting of words, they are aptly used for unaccented syllables; they serve well in the presentation of tone-colour for its own sake, through their lack of any positive harmonic quality; as temporary resting-points where finality is not desired; or as the incidental by-products of movement and of the combination of melodies. They are as useful in music as is the colour grey in painting.

# CHAPTER FOURTEEN

# NON-REGULAR CHORD STRUCTURE

## II

### DISSONANT GROUPINGS

IN THIS SECOND CATEGORY of empirical chord-shapes there is even less definable method of building than in that of neutral chords. The only common factor among these infinitely varied groupings is the presence of one or more dissonant components of the strongest type, the minor seconds or ninths, or the major sevenths. A definition as broad as this would include some classical chords, such as the minor ninth and those secondary-seventh chords whose sevenths are major; and it would also include the countless combinations which are by-products of contrapuntal, parallel, or pattern movements. Almost any random reference to examples throughout this book will remind us of the almost constant presence of the stronger discords, and of the overlapping of procedures which precludes cut and dried analysis. With this qualification, the general division into concordant, neutral, and dissonant groupings has value in so far as it points to a changed aesthetic attitude to discord. The traditional idea was that of temporary departure from a norm; the current one, in the work of many composers, is akin to distortion in the visual arts; it is an inevitable part of the artist's reaction as he perceives or conceives new forms of order. Emphasis on the *fact* of discord (or distortion), is the point which emerges strongly, and the different means of securing such discord can be found in association with any and every type of harmony.

Any general principle governing this technique must also cover the continuous absorption of new resources and of discord into general harmonic experience. Such a principle indeed might well be stated as one of resistance to absorption. Earlier (see p. 63) a criterion was proposed for estimating the harmonic stability of groups produced by decoration, that of intelligibility through association with what is already familiar. To perceive logical relations with already ordered sounds is to go far towards accepting accompanying discord. Transitional developments took place against a background of triad harmony. Later the environment became far more varied; but as long as recognizable order prevails in a context, discord will appear as an attendant feature rather than as an end in itself. Several examples already given illustrate this secondary role (36*a* and *b*, 37, 41, 46, 50, concerned with decoration of triads; 60*a*, illustrating a parallel-interval strand; 63, dealing with pattern; and 97, 100, arising from equal-interval structure of chords). The influence of established order underlying diatonic music should also be noted in this connexion. Thus in Ex. 107*a*, more dissonant intervals appear on the bass stave in bar 6, but in the diatonic context they differ only slightly from the prevailing neutral chords.

The deliberate search for discord involves the avoidance of these recognizable associations. In the case of triad harmony normal identity is effectively avoided, for instance, by the conflict of major and minor third (as in Ex. 33, and in Ex. 95*c*); and in the case of seventh-chords and further structures in thirds, it is not only the presence of a dissonant interval which heightens tension, but rather the spacing (*e.g.* the first chord of Ex. 30*a*), and the new inter-relations of sub-groups in the texture (Ex. 96). Similarly, when decoration is added to traditional harmony, the ear will accept groupings of notes in proportion as their treatment follows traditional lines. Thus in Ex. 108*a* the first chord could be described as an appoggiatura to the second, and it could easily occur in a classical context. Yet that first chord contains, in its upper three notes, exactly the same group as that seen at 1 in Ex. 100*b*, where it has a most acutely dissonant effect, since attention is focussed there on its dissonant interval constitution, not on its logical relation to a familiar chordal environment. Again, bars 3 and 5 should be compared. In this case there is a more acute dissonance on the first beat of bar 5, where the major seventh A-G sharp is present instead of the A-G natural of bar 3, but there is also a strange unfamiliarity in the lack of connexion between the melody of bar 5 and its accompanying chord, which did not exist in the conventional decoration of bar 3.

In contrast to the first chord of Ex. 108*a*, the appoggiatura chords at 108*b* have much more bite, since each of their notes sounds simultaneously with the harmony note it would traditionally have displaced. This effect is intensified in the second chord, where the appoggiaturas affect the bass and the harmony notes sound simultaneously above. The decorative groups here are plain triads. At first sight, the decorative figuration of 108*c* might appear to involve fairly strong

Ex. 108 SCHÖNBERG *Das Buch der hängenden Gärten* No. 10

Music extract reprinted by arrangement with Universal Edition A.G. Vienna
(Alfred A. Kalmus, London)

VAUGHAN WILLIAMS Fourth Symphony,
fourth movement

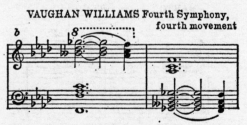

Music extract reprinted by permission of the
publishers, Oxford University Press

(Ex. 108) WALTON  *Belshazzar's Feast*

Music extract reprinted by permission of the
publishers, Oxford University Press

friction, but it is actually very readily absorbed into the total
dominant seventh chord shown at *d*.    A vast amount of
decorative and contrapuntal discord has been so absorbed, as a
part of and continuation of classical procedure.

Applying the criterion of association with previous practice,
it is easy to see that the 'added note' method of chord-structure
is a simple device for securing the sensation of discord if
semitones are used, or if major sevenths are incorporated.  Such
groupings have had no previous function in the course of
harmonic evolution, and their impact is correspondingly fresh.
They were also correspondingly exploited in the first onrush
of twentieth-century discord.   (Some typical groupings are
quoted at 108*i*, from Stravinsky's *Sacre du Printemps*.)   Apart,
however, from that fashionable use of discord, a sense of
relative values is discernable in its employment, and the device,

BARTOK  *Bluebeard's Castle*

Music extract reprinted by arrangement
with Universal Edition (London) Ltd.

no worse for being simple, can have a true function in twentieth-century harmony.   Ex. 108e, from Bartok's *Bluebeard's Castle* reflects in its semitonal addition to the basic triad a new shock of foreboding experienced by Judith; and one of the tensest harmonic moments in Kodaly's *Psalmus Hungaricus*, at the words 'violence and strife', is contrived by adding a biting little strand of major sevenths to a tremolando major-cum-minor thirds basis.   Similarly *f* derives its melodic shape and

WALTON  *Belshazzar's Feast*

Music extract reprinted by permission of the publishers, Oxford
University Press

its taut semitone interval from the idea of the accompanying words 'Babylon is fallen'; in bars 2 and 3 the semitone emerges as an isolated interval, and in the last two chords it occurs in association with reminiscent shapes of harmony.   The idea of relative degrees of tension, this time without verbal associations, is illustrated by the varied accompaniment at *g* and *h*, where the initial statement and then the recapitulation of a theme are shown.   The examples at *i* show dissonant intervals incorporated into more complex combinations, though still on a triadic basis.

In the same way the exploiting of dissonant possibilities can be studied in the various forms of post-classical harmony already examined.   The 'discordant' additions to whole-tone harmony seen in Ex. 51a were sufficiently remote from current experience in 1902 to make their impact notable.   The intervals chosen for parallel use in Ex. 57h, and at *b* and *c* in Ex. 59, are strongly dissonant in themselves, not merely passing discords.

(Ex.108) BARTOK Second String Quartet, first movement

Music extracts reprinted by arrangement with Universal Edition(London) Ltd.

Again, the pattern progressions at C and E in Ex. 71 are designed to culminate in deliberately tense conjunctions; and varying degrees of tension are to be seen among the regular chord-structures in Exs. 96, 97, 100.

However closely such analysis of dissonance may be pursued, no ultimate judgment can be based on merely grammatical tests. Musical thought is communicated as a whole in a succession of ordered sounds; and the place of a harmonic group in relation to that whole must be considered as well as the details of its vertical construction.* This is true perhaps most of all in the matter of tension, since time is required for a

---

*This point emerges clearly in Hindemith's system, as presented in his *Craft of Musical Composition*. He gives there a classification of chords at three main levels, and a further subdivision of each of these classes into those which include the indeterminate tritone interval and those which do not. Progression between chords of these six classes involves rise or fall of harmonic tension, which can be assessed by reference to the scale of harmonic values indicated in Series 2 (shown in Ex. 83b, page 131). But in addition to this purely chordal aspect of progression, and its tonal organization by root-relationships, Hindemith builds up a detailed synthesis in which he postulates a close correspondence between melodic and harmonic climax and repose; and so he recognizes the interdependence and the relative nature of all the elements of composition.

STRAVINSKY 'Jeu du Rapt' from *Sacre du Printemps*

Music extract reprinted by permission of Boosey & Hawkes Ltd.

process of growth and relaxation to be apparent. Nevertheless, although chord-structure is only one of many contributory factors, sharply dissonant intervals will clearly play a dominant part in the processes of securing harmonic tension. This

Ex.109  BARTOK  Fourth String Quartet, fourth movement

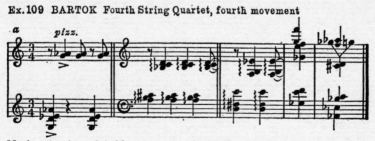

Music extract reprinted by arrangement with Universal Edition(London) Ltd.

RAWSTHORNE   Concerto for String Orchestra, first movement

Music extract reprinted by permission of the publishers, Oxford
University Press

general classification may therefore be completed by reference to combinations primarily designed for their quality of discord. Two approaches are illustrated in Ex. 109, vertical at *a*, and more contrapuntal at *b*. The pizzicato string chords of the first example are percussive clusters used primarily as accompaniment, though it should be recalled that semitones are thematically important in this quartet.   In the following example, the placing of the upper and lower parts in relation to one another has a controlling influence in the harmony (minor ninths and major sevenths predominating); and this outline is filled in partly with triads and partly with dissonant intervals (at the points marked X).

Here again the point is approached where harmony is derived from part-movement, and the chord as such has no meaning as an isolated vertical structure.

# CHAPTER FIFTEEN

# NON-REGULAR CHORD-STRUCTURE
# III

## COMPOSITE HARMONY

BEFORE FINALLY taking leave of harmonic groups analysable apart from a melodic context, we must glance at a large borderland of harmony not contrapuntal in origin and yet not completely static in conception. Unlike the traditional chord, which was a complete entity in itself, this harmony is of a composite nature, and its particular characteristic is that it requires time for its separate elements to be presented.

Certain kinds of pedal harmony possess this character, which may appear in two forms. In the first, the pedal itself consists of separate elements which are in motion and which by their interplay produce a kind of harmonic oscillation. An early example can be seen is the contrary-motion trill in Beethoven's Op. 90 sonata (shown at Ex. 76). It is recalled here at Ex. 110a for comparison with a more recent application of the device at b, which illustrates its common use to secure a steady friction of dissonance, F sharp and G natural being placed in constant opposition. One more example is added, at 110c, showing an internal pedal formed by a broad alternation of two chords, a harmonic ostinato.

In the second form of pedal harmony, the pedal itself is a stationary element, and additions are made which combine with it to form a composite harmonic whole. This principle is well established in classical practice, but its application in twentieth-century music presents new features. Thus where classical or romantic harmony would revert to triadic structure after its temporary expansion to include the foreign pedal element, a twentieth-century texture would be quite likely to incorporate the pedal into a composite whole, explicable only

Ex. 110 BEETHOVEN  Piano Sonata, Opus 90, second movement

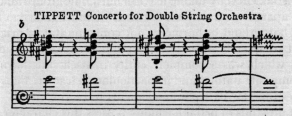

TIPPETT  Concerto for Double String Orchestra

Music extract reprinted by permission of Schott & Co. Ltd.

in its own context.  Ex. 111 illustrates this process.  At *a*, the contrary motion of the upper and lower strands, added to the E chord which persists throughout in the middle parts, leads to a tritonal chord in the second bar, fully accepted in its own right, and quitted without 'resolution'.  A longer process, at *b*, leads to the building up by stages of a chord which is approximately a fifth-structure, but with differences which are clearly accounted for by the successive additions to the initial pedal group.

A third example is given at *c* to show that apparently complex textures of this kind may have a simple foundation. The same bar, seen at *d* without its added semitones, appears more clearly as two melodic strands against an internal pedal. The feature which does call for comment is the interval-structure of the sub-groups in the harmony, semitones in this case being prominent.  At the risk of tedious repetition we must

SCHÖNBERG *Das Buch der hängenden Gärten*, No. 8

Music extract reprinted by arrangement with Universal Edition A.G.
(Alfred A. Kalmus, London)        Vienna

Ex.111 RAWSTHORNE Concerto for
String Orchestra, third movement

Music extract reprinted by permission of
the publishers, Oxford University Press

(Ex.111) BRITTEN *The Rape of Lucretia*, Act II, Scene Two (Outline only)

Music extract reprinted by permission of Boosey & Hawkes Ltd.

refer once again to the matter of characteristic intervals, since
a pedal is obviously a useful nucleus about which to assemble
individual elements intended to make their own special effect.
Another example, clearly designed to preserve in the harmonic
context the influence of a striking major seventh in the previous
melody, should be referred to in Ex. 118c.

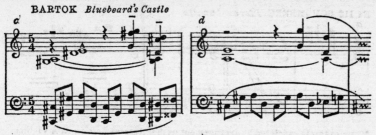

BARTOK  *Bluebeard's Castle*

Music extracts reprinted by arrangement with Universal Edition (London) Ltd.

The setting of two chords in relationship to complete a harmonic effect is further seen in what may be called 'quasi-appoggiatura' groups, a term used to distinguish them from appoggiatura chords in the strict sense. The classical appoggiatura is a form of decoration applied to a basic chord which has its own separate existence. (Ex. 41 illustrates this usage.) The point of the present form of composite harmony is that neither group is a basic chord; they exist together on equal terms, as part of a single conception. Their function is often to secure dissonant friction (112*a*), and their influence in counteracting any tendency towards block harmony is seen at 112*b*. The contrast with chordal harmony is apparent if the classical appoggiatura technique (as seen at 3 and 4 in 112*c*) is substituted for the quasi-appoggiatura groups 1 and 2 in the Schönberg example. Instances of such pairings abound in modern music, both in isolation, as in the first examples of 112*a*, and in full and complex textures. They suggest a compromise between the vertical and the horizontal aspects of music, and from this point of view, the two 'false relation' examples, 112*d* and *e*, though not showing quite the same appoggiatura relationship, share the general characteristic of composite harmony: the groups must be taken as a pair, and cannot make their harmonic effect alone.

A final application of the principle of unfolding harmony is seen in Ex. 113. Such situations have long been common in pianoforte writing. When the spread of the harmony exceeds the stretch of the hands, one part of a chord is played first and

Ex.112 SCHÖNBERG *Pierrot Lunaire*

Music extracts reprinted by arrangement with Universal Edition A.G. Vienna
(Alfred A. Kalmus, London)

SCHÖNBERG Six Little Piano Pieces, Opus 19, No. 5

Music extracts reprinted by arrangement with Universal Edition A.G. Vienna
(Alfred A. Kalmus, London)

retained by the pedal and other parts added when the hand becomes free. The new feature here is that the total group finally produced is not a definable chord, as it would have been in earlier times. The harmony is composite, and it acquires an unusually variegated character since sub-groups, which would have an aggressive effect if sounded simultaneously, are far more easily assimilated when heard in succession and previous

BARTOK Second String Quartet, third movement

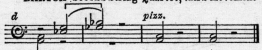

Music extract reprinted by arrangement with Universal
Edition (London) Ltd.

WALTON Viola Concerto, first movement

Music extract reprinted by permission of the publishers,
Oxford University Press

impressions have been given time to fade. Comment on the
examples is unnecessary, except in the case of *d*, which could
be described as a ninth-chord on A flat, with three unresolved
appoggiaturas, as indicated at *e*.

Ex.113 SCHÖNBERG Six Little Piano Pieces, Opus 19, No. 6

Music extract reprinted by arrangement with Universal
Edition A.G. Vienna (Alfred A. Kalmus, London)

SCHÖNBERG *Pierrot Lunaire*

Music extract reprinted by arrangement with Universal
Edition A.G. Vienna (Alfred A. Kalmus, London)

(Ex.113) SCHÖNBERG  Three Piano Pieces, Opus 11, No. 3

Music extract reprinted by arrangement with Universal
Edition A.G. Vienna (Alfred A. Kalmus, London)

LENNOX BERKELEY  Six Preludes, No.1

Music extracts reprinted by permission of J.&W. Chester Ltd.

# CHAPTER SIXTEEN

# INTER-RELATION OF MELODY
# AND HARMONY

TURNING FROM ANALYSIS of chord-structure in isolation to the consideration of harmony as part of a musical context, we encounter again the principle of movement. Harmony only acquires its fullest meaning in association with melody and rhythm, since the nature of music is to unfold in time. Stress on its vertical aspects was a characteristic of a comparatively brief period, the last three centuries of European music; and although a wealth of resource was developed during that time, a better perspective of the varied possibilities in texture can be obtained by recalling some characteristic types of earlier ages. Briefly, these have included unharmonized melody, such as plainsong and folk-song (to which may be added the duplicated melody of Organum); combined melodies maintaining considerable independence over most of their course, as in early polyphony; combined melodies with systematic interval relationship and control of dissonance, in later polyphony; and finally the phase of chordal dominance of the texture, which has been broadly defined as classical in this study.

In varying degrees these different techniques have been consciously revived by twentieth-century composers. They are coloured of course by the accumulated experience of successive centuries. Organum-like strands are woven of latter-day chords and intervals, melodic shapes adapt themselves to twelve-note instead of diatonic contours, drone basses become sophisticated ostinatos or pedal harmonies. The influence of accumulated experience expresses itself also in a negative way, in the avoidance of the flavour of classical harmony and of traditional degrees of consonance and blend. Whole works of the 'neo-classical' kind come to mind as examples. The opening of Stravinsky's Octet for Wind Instruments, Ex. 114*a*, recalls the style. The work throughout has its own positive qualities of instrumental lucidity; but one of its specific harmonic characteristics is its frequent negation of classical convention in the grammar underlying its turns of speech.

However the details may change, the principles underlying these forms of organization remain, and the twentieth-century attitude to harmony in general (*i.e.*, to musical texture in depth), can well be illustrated by the varied interpretations which those principles have received. For the most part these depend on different kinds of interplay among melodies themselves, but some final aspects of chordal harmony may be observed before the completely contrapuntal ones are examined.

### Melody and Chordal Harmony

This relationship may be expressed in two main ways. The first, the harmonization of a melody, is familiar in classical tradition, and it also provides the framework within which

Ex. 114 STRAVINSKY Octet for Wind Instruments

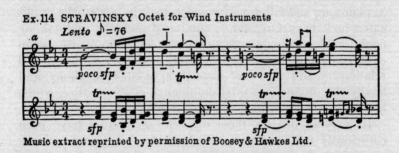

Music extract reprinted by permission of Boosey & Hawkes Ltd.

many modern resources are used. The choice of appropriate harmony is a factor in composition, but one technical aspect assumes importance in view of the heterogeneous nature of the materials now available. Selection from these widely contrasted resources and maintenance of consistency in their use presents a more teasing problem of style today than ever before. There is considerable latitude in practice, and there is also fascinating concentration in method. Bartok, in his Violin Concerto for

BARTOK Violin Concerto, first movement

Music extract reprinted by permission of Boosey & Hawkes Ltd.

example, harmonizes a melody strongly characterized by
fourths in one case by an accompaniment of fourth-chords (see
Ex. 98*f*), in another case in the same movement by a completely independent triadic accompaniment (Ex. 114*b*); and
in a third case a melody of fourths together with a counter-
melody move independently against a pedal background
(Ex. 114*c*). On the other hand, in the Fourth String Quartet,
he maintains a consistent homogeneity of texture in both horizontal and vertical respects, while securing at the same time
subtle distinctions of character between movements, by
emphasis now on one interval, now on another. Brief quotations from this work occur at Exs. 97, 102*f*, 109*a*, and 118*b*.
Schönberg, in his early *Kammer Symphonie* (1906), uses such
widely divergent resources as post-Wagnerian decorative

chromaticism, unrelieved whole-tone harmony, sections of fourth-chords and melody, in succession and also in some degree of combination. In contrast with this essay, with its unassimilated materials, works like *Pierrot Lunaire*, and *Das Buch der hängenden Gärten* are models of stylistic individuality and coherence.

Such general examples can be multiplied indefinitely and no consistent technical system of matching melody and harmony can be deduced from them. Sharply contrasting units of harmony present their respective melodic facets in bewildering variety; each individual composer makes his own selection and his own synthesis. Two age-old principles, the contrapuntal control of movement and the increase and release of tension, continue their governing influence. Two other factors acquire particular prominence in the absence of any ready-made harmonic system: the composer's flair for sound-combinations, and his skill in presenting them in the chosen medium. It is scarcely possible to refer to this aspect of harmony without recalling Stravinsky's contribution. In style his approach is personal; but in this strictly musical field of imagination and invention in pure sound he touches the central problem of contemporary technique.

The second kind of relation between melody and chordal harmony is characterized by some degree of active interplay between the two elements. A simple example is the traditional appoggiatura. This involves a melodic movement against a stationary basis, and as long as the discord lasts a combination is produced which is not analysed simply as a chord but as a temporary interplay of melody and harmony. This principle, flexibly expanded, underlies the examples which follow. The appoggiatura relationship itself is suggested at Ex. 115a, in the movement of the two chords on the lower stave, but there is a strong separative tendency between melody and chords, which is exploited bitonally in the succeeding context. Again at *b* the notes played by the oboe may be regarded as appoggiaturas to the chord of A in the strings, but actual resolution is not made, and the idea emerges of chord and melody set in independent and slightly frictional relationship.

Ex. 115 BARTOK *Bluebeard's Castle*

BRITTEN *Spring* Symphony, Part III *Fair and fair*

(The first bar of Ex. 118c shows a discordant relationship of this kind employed for a descriptive purpose in setting poignant words.) The loosening of links between decoration and basic harmony was seen in Chapter Three to facilitate free chordal juxtapositions in the horizontal sense of chords in succession.

The same process can lead to considerable freedom in vertical juxtapositions. Thus in the quotation at 115*c* the upper strand has a decorative origin, and the appoggiatura groups on the first beats of bars 2 and 3 could easily be resolved diatonically. Instead of that, Ravel follows the bitonal suggestion set up by the right-hand group in bar 2, and explores some remote harmonic combinations with the basic pedal on F.

(Ex.115) RAVEL   *Valse Nobles et Sentimentales*, No. VII

Music extract reprinted by permission of Durand & Cie.

The decorative method has been used as an illustration of the idea of interplay between melody and chordal harmony. It is obviously only one of many methods, in view of the copious resources available in chord-structure and in progression of strands within a texture. The principle of interaction is in fact fully established in twentieth-century music, in the sense that there is a completely free choice of relationships designed for dissonance or for securing new forms of order. It may be applied throughout long passages. Ex. 116*a* shows the harmonic organization of a complete section, lasting some forty bars, in Britten's *Spring Symphony*, and the passage of accompaniment from Lennox Berkeley's oratorio *Jonah*, seen at *b*,

Ex. 116 BRITTEN *Spring* Symphony, Part I, *Spring, the sweet spring*

Spring, the sweet    spring, the sweet spring    is    the

years    plea - sant    king

Music extract reprinted by permission of Boosey & Hawkes Ltd.

LENNOX BERKELEY *Jonah*

Music extracts reprinted by permission of J. & W. Chester Ltd.

persists for several bars. (Whether this is a form of composite
pedal harmony of the kind illustrated in Ex. 110, or whether
there is a deliberate reversal of the conventional chords given
at 116c is open to conjecture.) A most telling placing of a
bass ostinato in relationship to chordal harmony is shown at

116*d*, and the two extracts at 116*e* indicate the technical means employed by Vaughan Williams to achieve the elusive harmony of the last movement of his Sixth Symphony: partly

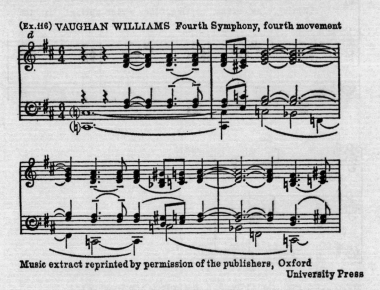

(Ex.116) VAUGHAN WILLIAMS Fourth Symphony, fourth movement

Music extract reprinted by permission of the publishers, Oxford
University Press

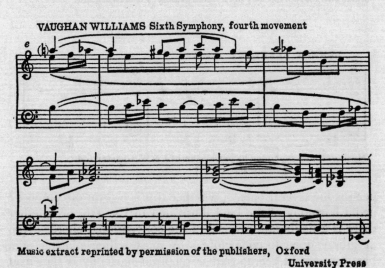

VAUGHAN WILLIAMS Sixth Symphony, fourth movement

Music extract reprinted by permission of the publishers, Oxford
University Press

dissonant placing of individual melodic lines, partly dissonant
relationship between chord and melody.

The triad, an apparently inexhaustible source of musical
experience in one new guise after another, provided the basis
of the foregoing examples. A last quotation, 116*f* is added
to show that the simple principle of relationship may be the
controlling factor in textures of more complex appearance
than that of triadic harmony. The violin notes marked X and
Y have the same function in relation to their accompanying
pianoforte chords as the corresponding notes at *g* have in
relation to the hypothetical chordal scheme sketched there.
In the latter case they are appoggiaturas placed to secure
dissonance against defined chords in a key; in the former case
they hold a similar relative position, but against chords which

BARTOK  Second Violin Sonata

Music extracts reprinted by permission of the publishers, Oxford
University Press

(Ex. 116)

are constructed for percussive effect in themselves and also as a counterbalance to the general melodic phrase-shape.

A further aspect of the interplay between melody and harmony is to be observed, one in which the harmonic structure itself reflects in various degrees the influence of melody. The processes illustrated in Chapters Four and Five, in which decorative figuration and part-movements produced new chord-shapes and a new fluidity of texture, are carried forward in the work of this century and account for the form taken by a large amount of harmony. Some examples are given (117), which scarcely depart in principle from this ancient line of development; and yet in their fluid harmonic character they present features which defy chordal and decorative analysis.

Ex. 117 SCHÖNBERG *Das Buch der Hängenden Gärten* No. 14

Music extract reprinted by arrangement with Universal Edition A.G. Vienna
(Alfred A. Kalmus, London)

RICHARD STRAUSS *Don Quixote* Variation X

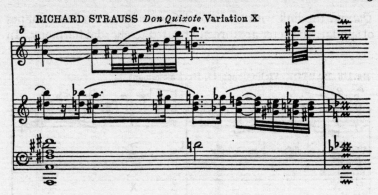

SCHÖNBERG *Das Buch der Hängenden Gärten* No. 1

Music extract reprinted by arrangement with Universal Edition A.G. Vienna
(Alfred A. Kalmus, London)

The typically Schönbergian texture of 117a cannot be viewed
as a broken chord or as decorative figuration applied to an
underlying basis, yet shapes that were formerly produced by
decoration make their impress on the harmony. Recalling
along with this passage the one at *b* from Strauss's *Don*

*Quixote*, the link with tradition becomes clear, for here, shapes of similar character are directly related to chordal harmony.  In

Ex.118 BARTOK Violin Concerto, first movement

Music extract reprinted by permission of Boosey & Hawkes Ltd.

BARTOK Fourth String Quartet, fifth movement

Music extract reprinted by arrangement with Universal Edition (London) Ltd.

Ex. 117*c* from the same work of Schönberg, the harmony is seen in a state of growth, by melodic movement outwards from the note E, first to the group at X, which forms the nucleus of a fourth chord, then with further expansion in bar 4 by continuation of the part-movement.

The examples at 117 show the flexibility of harmony in its

BRITTEN *The Rape of Lucretia* Act I, Scene Two

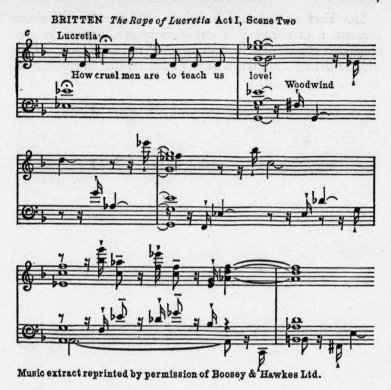

Music extract reprinted by permission of Boosey & Hawkes Ltd.

response to melodic movement, and in this respect they prepare
for a further stage of the penetration of harmony by melody.
This takes the form of the incorporation of salient melodic
features in the chordal structure. The chords at X in Ex.
118*a* reflect in their simultaneous major and minor thirds
the inflexions of the successive intervals in the violin melody.
At *b*, the characteristic Magyar scale notes are reproduced in
the accompaniment and so explain the chordal formation.
These instances show simultaneous occurrence of the same
features in melody and harmony. A final example, 118*c*,
shows a delayed action, a 'memory' of previously heard melody,
the major seventh on 'How cruel' being retained and incorporated in the harmonic texture.

This kind of interplay is clearly only possible when the conception of harmony is not a static one, limited to preconceived chords and their decoration, but an organic one, in which the harmonic language is freshly created in response to the musical thought.

# CHAPTER SEVENTEEN

# MELODIES IN COMBINATION

W E HAVE STUDIED the influence of horizontal movement
on the relations between melody and chordal
harmony; there remain to be observed some vertical
implications of twentieth-century methods in the purely
contrapuntal field.

The main historical types of melodic combination were
mentioned in the first paragraph of Chapter 16. These were
seen to vary in principle from free play of individual lines to
closely controlled inter-relations. Both extremes are touched in
modern work. The climax of harmonic expansion which was
reached between 1890 and 1910 owed much to a new conception of melody free from triadic association; but in those two
decades, emphasis on the vertical aspects of harmony, on new
shapes, new colours, new degrees of dissonance, largely pre-
dominated over contrapuntal views of texture. Nevertheless,
although obscured during that phase of preoccupation with
sonorous novelty, another conception did exist: that of the all-
sufficiency of melody itself. Here particularly may be seen a
lasting influence of the work of the Russian nationalists, notably
Mussorgsky; and also the results of an awakening interest in
primitive modes of expression. Some of its technical manifestations have been illustrated above, in the association of melody
with pedals and with ostinatos. A variant of this idea appears
in the practice known as heterophony illustrated in Ex. 115,
where in each case a single melody provides the material for
the separate parts in the texture. The parts make continuous
use of the same notes, which may or may not coincide in time,
and sound together with no organized form of vertical combination. In this respect, heterophony differs from the scholastic
devices of canon and augmentation, which in some ways it

O

superficially resembles. Portions of the one melody, combining with each other at varying points of contact, produce incidental harmonic effect which may vary from the average blend of 'neutral chord' harmony (119a), to passing frictions of a piquant nature (119b).

Ex. 119 STRAVINSKY Symphony of Psalms, first movement

Music extract reprinted by permission of Boosey & Hawkes Ltd.

In the same way, neutral harmony can be produced by combining different melodies. Ex 120 shows modal fragments at a, pentatonic at b. These melodies pursue independent courses, but the ease with which they blend illustrates the unceasing process of harmonic absorption. Just as free combination of melodies in early polyphony was ultimately superseded by the ordered relations of later polyphony, and the free declamation of the early Baroque era gave place to the classical synthesis of melody and triadic harmony, so diatonic melodies like those of Ex. 120 can form combinations which now pass as normal currency.

BARTOK Second String Quartet, second movement

Music extract reprinted by arrangement with Universal Edition (London) Ltd.

The tendency to absorption however meets conscious resistance. The pentatonic fragments at Ex. 120b, from Stravinsky's *Sacre du Printemps*, produce their own blend as a family, but they themselves are heard against a much more complex background. Various tonal planes are indicated in the extracts shown at 120b and c, all sounding simultaneously at this

Ex.120 VAUGHAN WILLIAMS *Pastoral* Symphony, Second movement

Music extract reprinted by permission of J. Curwen & Sons Ltd.

(Ex.120) STRAVINSKY   *Sacre du Printemps*

Music extracts reprinted by permission of Boosey & Hawkes Ltd.

point of climax in the prelude.  They are shown in compressed form at *d*.  The procedure illustrates another characteristic modern approach to the combination of elements in a texture, that of polytonality.  Here, in the *Sacre du Printemps* example, an

atmosphere is being built up which does not call for sharp differentiation between the thematic elements in the melodic and rhythmic sense. As these elements are gathered together, almost as a chorus of sounds in nature, the separate character which they do possess is underlined by harmonic and tonal separatism, as seen in 120d, rather than by the traditional methods of delineation. The latter approach, in contrast, is

TIPPETT  Concerto for Double String Orchestra, third movement

Music extract reprinted by permission of Schott & Co. Ltd.

SCHÖNBERG  *Pierrot Lunaire*

Music extract reprinted by arrangement with Universal Edition A.G. Vienna
(Alfred A. Kalmus, London)

illustrated in the finale of the *Jupiter* Symphony, where Mozart unites his five themes in the simplest chordal harmony while preserving their individuality, which springs from melody and rhythm.

Polytonality may be considered partly as an extension of contrapuntal practice—a sharpening of the edges of individual lines—and partly as a form of tonal organization. Used as a contrapuntal device, it does not of itself ensure definition of character in the separate melodic lines. These may each be in a different key (as for instance in Szymanowski's String Quartet Op. 37 and in a large miscellaneous literature of modern polytonal writing), but even so they may coalesce at times in harmonic blend and lose their identity in so far as this depends only on differentiation of key. Contrapuntal independence will rather depend upon the resistance to harmonic absorption, *i.e.*, upon the dissonant relations between the lines of the texture. The mutual relationships of the *Sacre du Printemps* quotation, as indicated at Ex. 120*d*, are significant.

As a method of tonal organization, polytonality has potentialities which again are suggested in the Stravinsky quotation at Exx. 120*b, c, d*. The final synthesis in the Prelude to the *Sacre* requires the placing of those thematic elements on different tonal levels. As those elements made their earlier appearances at those respective levels, the tonal scheme throughout the earlier stages was thus pre-ordained by the final polytonal requirements. The opposite process is indicated in the fugal procedure of Milhaud in No. 4 of his *Cinq Symphonies*, where he presents five successive subject entries in keys rising a fifth, each voice then retaining its key. In such a case polytonality would be rather a form of description than a method of organization. There is regular order in the procedure, but no guarantee that the resulting combination will have musical significance. It may have; but only as a product of factors which govern the whole work, not merely because each part is organized in a key of its own.

This qualification sets limits to the usefulness of polytonality as a method of tonal organization. It can give colour to sections of a work, but what is its effect if consistently applied throughout a movement? If any one key predominates, the traditional tonal method is in action; if the lead passes from one key to another, traditional modulation results; if the keys neutralize each other and a composite effect is attained, the key-system of tonal control is suspended and the method becomes once again empirical.

Whatever the object of polytonality, whether contrapuntal or structural, it carries with it harmonic implications. It presupposes horizontal listening of course, just as did the sixteenth century clashes of sharpened and unsharpened sevenths, but it provides opportunity for still another kind of adventure in vertical combination. At one extreme it gives rise to complex textures which are harmonically thick, though the resources of tone-colour and orchestration can be called upon to clarify the strands. But more productive of fresh harmonic experiences are the transparent contexts where the passing frictions between opposing tonalities can be more clearly heard. In this respect, the dual oppositions of bitonality are more effective than the larger polytonal combinations which contribute to general structure.

Some of the uses of bitonality are illustrated at Ex. 121. In the narrowest sense, the term implies the presence of two keys. Interpreted literally, this is an artificial limitation, and one not quite borne out in practice. We may include with classically definable keys those melodies of modal type, and even of nondiatonic type, which carry with them a strong suggestion of their own tonal centre. With this proviso, the examples at 121 are clearly bitonal. There is passing friction at *a*, and something like a continuous harmonic haze at *c*. The friction at *a* is not due so much to discord as to the crossing of one train of thought by another, which is obviously the defining feature of bitonality. (If the discord, E-E flat occurring in bar 2 is brought into one tonal plane as at *b* the special harmonic quality vanishes.) Although discord does not occur between simultaneous sounds in the opening phrase at *c*, it is strongly present if the harmonic implications of the broken chords are followed up. Compare the groups 1 and 2 at *d*; or alternatively, play the right-hand part of *c* without the flats. Again, Bartok's central cadence is shown at *e*, and its possible tonal equivalent at *f*. In this piece from the *Mikro-kosmos* there is clearly a strong suggestion of conscious experiment with centres a semitone apart. There is also a reminder, throughout the piece, of the importance of pitch and spacing, both in the inversion of the parts after the central cadence and in the recapitulation of the opening with the right hand an

Ex. 121 BARTOK   Fourteen Bagatelles, Opus 6, No. 1

Music extract reprinted by permission of Zenemükiadó Vállalat, Budapest

BARTOK   *Mikrokosmos*, No. 125

octave higher.   Ex. 121*g*, which closes the first movement of
Bloch's second string quartet, is especially effective in its
spacing of centres a semitone apart.

The example at *g*, moreover, illustrates a musically significant use of bitonality.   The character of its two separate
melodic strands is so arresting that there is clearly no need of
bitonal organization merely as an adventitious aid in accen-
tuating individual lines.   The musical effect depends on more
than the sum of their separate qualities; it derives from the
union of these two elements in a way that opens up a world of
remoteness and suggestion as opposed to one of matter-of-fact
statement.   (The opening and closing of the last movement of
Vaughan Williams's Pastoral Symphony have the same quality

Music extract reprinted by permission of Boosey & Hawkes Ltd.

BLOCH Second String Quartet, first movement

Music extract reprinted by permission of Boosey & Hawkes Ltd.

**(Ex. 121) VAUGHAN WILLIAMS** *Pastoral* **Symphony,**
first movement

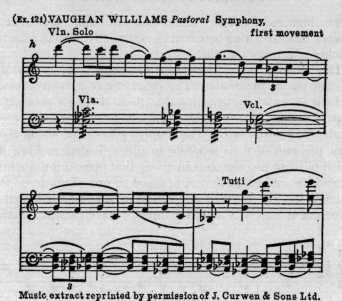

Music extract reprinted by permission of J. Curwen & Sons Ltd.

**BARTOK** *Bluebeard's Castle*

Music extract reprinted by arrangement with Universal Edition (London) Ltd.

and employ the same technique.) Certain musical experiences may be of a composite nature; their elements may have little logical inter-relation and may even appear to belong to different levels of consciousness. The communication of such an experience may be most aptly achieved through bitonal means. It may involve scarcely more obtrusiveness than is seen in the extract at 121*h*, from Vaughan Williams's Pastoral Symphony. Here indeed it would be difficult to define a specific 'key' in the lower chordal strand, which could rather be described as a triadic outlining of a melody (the upper notes of the triads), belonging to the same mode as the treble stave melody. Or it may employ sharp contrast, as at 121*i* from Bartok's *Bluebeard's Castle*, one of several bitonal textures arising from psychological situations in the opera. A more fleeting glimpse of dual relationships appears in the descending scale at 121*j*, where the note D, the third of the B flat triad, attracts the melody momentarily into the scale of D.

RAWSTHORNE Violin Concerto, second movement

Music extract reprinted by permission of the publishers, Oxford University Press

It would be fruitless to look for antecedents of bitonal practices in the normal growth of harmony before the late nineteenth century. Isolated instances, such as the false horn entry in the *Eroica* and the horn calls in Act II of *Tristan*—bi-chordal rather than bitonal—serve to stress the abnormality of the device before that period, and the fact that harmony, through all its decorative and contrapuntal vicissitudes, was conceived as a unity. As soon as this conception lost its universal validity and separate strands were commonly used to form a composite texture, it was natural that this resource, always latent in the triadic structure of chords (see page 151 and Ex. 94), should assume considerable prominence.

In the foregoing examples of modern texture arising from the free play of individual melodic lines, we have traced a fairly close correspondence to traditional tonal organization, at any rate in the separate parts. Innovation, in those cases, arose from the manner of combining the parts. To these groups should be added the textures produced by parallel and pattern movements, already illustrated in Chapters Seven and Eight, and the types of twelve-note melody discussed in Chapter Nine. Here, novelty in combination results from the new forms of order within the melodies themselves. (See for instance the counterpoint produced in Ex. 71 between figures 29 and 30.)

This is true also of music written in the Twelve-Note System, with its rigidity in contrapuntal combination arising from the exigencies of the tone-row. It is quite possible, in that system, to produce any desired degree of concord between the parts if inflexible maintenance of thematic detail in melody is sacrificed to harmonic blend. Berg's violin concerto, for example, reveals a wide variety of harmonic resource and range of emotional expression. Conversely, if thematic exactness is preserved in the melodic lines, vertical combinations cease to be open to free choice. In Ex. 84b, strict melodic imitation of this kind was maintained, and in 84c consistent interval patterns were preferred to euphony. The claim in such case for the complete 'emancipation of the discord' is understood to be in the interests of untrammelled contrapuntal scope.

A final assertion of the primacy of melody is seen in such a work as Stravinsky's *L'Histoire du Soldat*. This particular harmonic idiom, underlined by scoring which precludes the merging of lines into a chordal unity, is illustrated in the extract at Ex. 122 from the *Great Choral* in that work. The combination of melodies in the so-called Gothic polyphony of the post-Organum age is suggested by these lines, which move between successive cadences without specific inter-relation. Stravinsky's procedure differs, in principle, only by the fact that his texture derives something of its organization from lines defined by tone-colour.

At the opposite extreme to these new methods of combining

Ex. 122 STRAVINSKY 'Great Choral' from *L'Histoire du Soldat*

Music extract reprinted by permission of J. & W. Chester Ltd.

independent melodic lines, a counterpart to the polyphonic use of controlled intervals and dissonance exists in the dissonant counterpoint of the twentieth century. The parallel cannot be carried far, since discord in the earlier polyphony was used against the background of a definite norm of consonance, whereas in this century it has an entirely relative nature. Nevertheless, the essential feature of both these contrapuntal methods is that of combining melodies together by chosen intervals. Two purposes are thereby fulfilled: the adjustment of the norm of concord in each particular context, and the securing of rise and fall of tension in relation to that norm. Thomas Weelkes' madrigal, *O Care, thou wilt despatch me*,

Ex. 123 VAUGHAN WILLIAMS Fourth Symphony, first movement

Music extract reprinted by permission of the publishers, Oxford University Press

(Ex. 123) VAUGHAN WILLIAMS Fourth Symphony, fourth movement

BARTOK Fourth String Quartet, fourth movement

Music extract reprinted by arrangement with Universal Edition (London) Ltd.

reveals these contrasts with considerable force in 1600, in the standard of discord which is set in its poignant sections as compared with the consonance of its 'fa-las' and of its more consolatory words. Vaughan Williams's Fourth Symphony also announces in no uncertain terms at its opening (Ex. 123a) the mood of grimness which is to prevail, and provides an example within the work itself of gradation of discord and mounting tension (123b). The latter example includes chordal elements, although the overriding influence of its two outside parts is unmistakable; gradation of dissonance is seen in a fully contrapuntal texture in the placing of the intervals (marked X) at Ex. 123c, and it is to be observed at different levels throughout the movement. Of the remaining examples at 123, d and e show the use of traditional devices, the first one imitation and canon, the second one triple counterpoint, with normal modern dissonance; and the last at f (the opening of *Pierrot Lunaire*), besides indicating the high level of discord which is to pervade the whole work, reveals the extent to which the interplay of lines and tone-colours can replace the chordal conception of harmony.

WELLESZ Fifth String Quartet

Music extract reprinted by permission of Schott & Co. Ltd.

# CHAPTER EIGHTEEN

# CONCLUSION

A T THE BEGINNING of this study we set out to discover why twentieth-century music sounds so unlike earlier music; and certain processes have been examined in order to find an answer. If a listener is prepared to make such technical analysis, how much will his response to music be facilitated? His curiosity will be satisfied, but the question may still be asked: 'Is it necessary to understand the technical workings? May not a preoccupation with mechanical details be a distraction in an art which demands more than a mere intellectual co-operation between composer and listener?'

A purely technical approach is of course incomplete. It could even be conceded that an uninformed but sensitive listener may come closer to a balanced view of much of the music of any period than a merely technically expert Beckmesser. But there are certain conditions present in twentieth-century music which make unusual demands on the listener's awareness of technical method. Music written in the Twelve-note system is an obvious example. Here is a newly created convention; and although the structural problems involved may be regarded as the composer's own concern, there are, as in chess, moves which need to be known if the strategy is to be appreciated by the observer. Here also the listener must abandon certain assumptions about music: euphony he may already have ceased to expect, and tonality is excluded by definition.

Apart from this extreme case there is still a wide field of music in which previous expectations have to be corrected by knowledge, and former associations resisted. Melody, in particular, must be judged in its new non-diatonic setting. Many now innocuous intervals in earlier times have had

emotional significance or heightened tension in relation
to a diatonic norm. As other standards replace that norm,
appreciation of the musical thought is correspondingly
affected. The listener must be able to trace the new curves of
melodies and respond to variations of tension against the
changed background. Unless he can perceive the new forms
of order, he is likely to attribute neurotic restlessness to much
modern melody and so misjudge its musical significance.

In the same way he must adjust himself to the new methods
of harmonic and contrapuntal organization, for aesthetic and
not only for technical reasons. The processes of evolution from
the triad to any twelve-note combination are easy enough to
follow and to accept, at least in theory; but a deliberate act of
'tuning-in' is involved when music itself is to be heard. The
amount of adjustment necessary is apparent if a few typical
textures are recalled. The triad itself, in its simplest guise, is
called upon by Vaughan Williams to produce musical atmos-
pheres varying from the stillness of the slow movement of the
*London* symphony (page 127), to the concentrated tension of
the fourth symphony (page 181). Additions to the triad, which
would be called decorative or unessential notes in classical
theory, have the musical function in *Belshazzar's Feast*, or *Bluebeard's Castle* (Ex. 108c and e, page 182), of temporarily
intensifying the existing harmonic norm. Those at Ex. 104i
are a measure of the far more persistently dissonant average
appropriate to the primitivism of the *Sacre du Printemps*. The
opening bars of this early ballet (page 126), contrasted with
the austere sounds of the *Orpheus* ballet (page 177), give
another glimpse of the widely differing textures opened up by
non-triadic harmony.

In these types of texture the composer is indicating the
norm of consonance and something of the average type of
combination and progression to be expected in a particular
movement. It remains for the listener to follow the clues. He
may learn to do this by the kind of grammatical analysis undertaken in this book, or he may do it by repeated hearings in the
course of which he stores up a multitude of aural experiences
which help him in each new work that he hears. Whatever

P

his method, he must now go further to meet the composer than in the past, since there is no ready-made medium of communication, no predetermined order in the materials of music. The composer is no longer working within an established convention, but creating his own language to express his musical thought. He must achieve intelligible order and the listener must recognize it, in each separate work.

If such difficulties in communication can be overcome, how far is the listener in a position to appreciate the music of the twentieth century? The purpose of this book has been to show that, underlying all the changes in detail, there has been continuity in the organization of musical textures. Melody, harmony, and rhythm still meet together in a synthesis. However new in feature and widened in scope, these elements can be judged by criteria of quality, now as in the past. A plainsong melody, a folk-song, a melody by Bach or a melody by Bartok can be enjoyed subjectively; they can also be judged objectively: and the same is true of harmony and rhythm. Old standards can also be used in judging the balance and interplay of these three elements. A fugue from Hindemith's *Ludus Tonalis*, like one from Bach's 48, will depend for its character on a subject of individual melodic and rhythmic stamp, which will be shown in various contrapuntal and tonal relationships. The only difference in method of musical organization lies in the diatonic basis of the earlier and the twelve-note basis of the later work. The significance achieved in either case would be judged by a common musical standard. A string quartet like Bloch's No. 2 differs from Beethoven's Op. 131 more in the details of its sound-combinations than in the basic method of presenting its musical thought. As with Bach and Hindemith, the essential musical approach is the same beneath the surface differences.

The two types of work just quoted recall a distinction made at the outset of this study between the expressive and the non-expressive views of the function of music. The divergent tendencies can occur, as they did in the past, in the work of the same composer. Thus Bach's fascinating designs, in Fugues, Suites, Inventions can be set against the glowing expression of

religious devotion in the Passions and Cantatas. Something of
the same duality appears in the change from expressive warmth
in the earlier Bartok to structural preoccupations as in the
third, fourth, and fifth String quartets. More marked by far
is the re-orientation of Stravinsky from the pre-1914 ballets to
the Neo-Classicism which became defined with his 1923 Octet.
Lavish in novel resources as those earlier works are, they may
still be interpreted technically in terms of the old synthesis of
melody, harmony, and rhythm; but the later works, though so
patently using the superficial materials of the classical past,
bring with them new aesthetic implications. Schönberg too
swings from one pole to the other, but although his course
takes him from the position of a decadent German romantic to
that of an 'Okeghem redivivus', his orbit virtually keeps within
the traditional range of the triple synthesis. The only qualification in his case is that so far as he makes contrapuntal demands
in some of his works at the expense of vertical considerations,
the synthesis is by that amount out of balance. His creative
imagination in harmony is witnessed both by his own earlier
expressive and descriptive works, and by the influence he
exerted on pupils and followers. Among these, Berg showed
how deeply his roots struck into musical tradition; they were
not artificially fed from merely cerebral sources.

The two extremes are represented by the later Schönberg
and the later Stravinsky. The main twentieth-century stream
has flowed with less self-conscious technical and aesthetic
effort in the work of groups nourished by their own national
cultures. Thus Vaughan Williams and Walton in particular
are able and willing to be naturally expressive and react to the
life about them with strong individual personality, fully within
the terms of pure music and the symphonic tradition. In the
significance of their thematic material and in power of sustained
thought they stand at the head of a fascinatingly varied and
numerous array of British composers, having affinities at one
extreme with the folk and Tudor past, in the centre with the
European tradition enriched in varying degree by native poetry
and vigour, and at the other extreme with the French school,
both through its teaching and its example. The Gallic spirit has

been active in this century, revealing itself even in the first flush of Impressionist music in a restraining taste and sense of style, and in austerer days which followed in poise and detachment. This influence has latterly been less in the direction of technical expansion than of aesthetic exploration. New views about music, clarification of the pure sound-materials of music, have come from France, and the Stravinsky who became French. The measure of this swing away from German predominance, which had been taken so much for granted since the eighteenth century, is given by the position of Hindemith. In his music, the essentially German tradition lives on, cooler after the abatement of the romantic fever, but true to type in a workmanlike presentation of sounds as 'links in a chain of thought'.

Between the extremes of the expressive and non-expressive, the emotional and the intellectual, the central stream flows on as always, the opposite qualities showing themselves in varying degrees of fusion and separatism. For the present writer, the composer who points the way most clearly in this direction is Bartok. He investigated new forms of order, his instinct as a musician gave them significance, whether heard purely as sound or viewed as symbols of thought and feeling. This has been the composer's function in all ages. At the present time, the point to be stressed is the *new* forms of order; and by using them imaginatively yet keeping a middle course, Bartok ensured his place in the line of succession and inspired confidence in his authority as a guide into the future.

What evidence does a study of contemporary harmony provide of possible development in the future? As far as technical evolution is concerned, an impasse seems to have been reached even in the first decade of the century. Among twelve undifferentiated semitones, choice must be arbitrary, and no universal musical convention can take the place once held by modal or major-minor scale systems. If no clue can be found, therefore, in the physical nature of music, possible developments can only arise from changes in personal idiom and outlook. Aesthetic re-alignments are in the nature of changes of fashion, subject to unaccountable fluctuation; they

afford no bearings by which a course can be plotted into the
future. Who, before the 1914 war, in the world of Stravinsky's
ballets, Schönberg's *Gurrelieder*, Debussy's and Strauss's tone-
poems, would have entertained a thought of the Neo-Classicism which was to open up in the 1920's a new world—or
perhaps a microcosm—into which the composer might with-
draw, turning from the riotous splendours of his recent past to
contemplation and practice of the purest ritual of his art?
This particular development was not foreseen, in spite of the
obvious clue provided by Satie's 'aberrations' and his ironic
detachment in the early century while the new-found powers
of harmony were being exploited. Nor was it of the least importance that, as a fashion, it should be foreseen. It has added to
the twentieth-century repertoire some works of coolness and
clarity which for many people are closer to the true spirit of
music than any other. But its possible contribution to the
future can best be estimated by some technical features which
they possess in common. On the negative side, the use of
material from earlier styles with the 'wrong' note, 'wrong'
spacing, 'wrong' resolution approach is a mark of fashion.
On the positive side, the preoccupation with form, not merely as
appropriate presentation of musical thought but for its own
sake, marks much of the work of the mid-century in matters of
structure and craftsmanship. This influence may well persist
in the coming years.

The insistence upon the intrinsic quality of sounds for
their own sake, rather than for their 'meaning', can have value
for the future composer in as much as harmony is chosen
empirically and not on existing chordal foundations. This
truly musical pre-occupation is not a monopoly of the Neo-
classic school, as varied works attest: Britten's operatic use of
orchestral sound, Bartok's variations in the slow movement of
the violin concerto, Vaughan Williams' imaginative con-
ceptions in the Sinfonia Antartica. How much of this sonorous
sense we owe to the fastidious and the purist can only be
guessed; but whatever its origin it seems likely to be a continuing influence in the future. How much its claims may be
reconciled with those of the opposite camp, with their ruthlessly

'emancipated dissonance', is an interesting speculation. Shall we some day listen to a musical discussion conducted in a Twelve-note language, but in Stravinskyan tones of voice? *

Neo-classicism implies withdrawal into a purely musical world. The opposite impulse is reflected in subjects sordid (*Wozzek, Lulu*), macabre (*Erwartung*), eccentric (*Pierrot Lunaire*), primitive (*Sacre du Printemps*), exotic (*Padmavati*); in jazz and in drawing-room pleasantries. In such works music embraces the particular and transitory; it shows a concern with events of the moment, and to that extent it is subject to chance and to change.

Drawing-room pleasantries certainly suggest the transitory. In the sense that they are 'sophisticated', thrive on allusion and under-statement and involve correspondingly elliptical musical processes, they contribute too, however unpretentiously, to new forms of order and new relationships. In this respect their contribution is the same in principle as that which comes from less elegant sources. The neurotic, the psychologically un-balanced, and the rest, reveal disorder in relation to the human average. For the dramatist, or the composer, this very dis-order is a challenge to explore new relationships, both psycho-logically and in the technical terms of their art. The 'human tragedies' involve a higher degree of tension than the witticisms of drawing-room art, but in both cases there is an urge to explore new forms of order.

To attempt a prediction of such new forms in art is to attempt to predict individual human conduct. If there is one parallel between art and life which emerges from this survey of the position of music in the twentieth century it is suggested by the word 'relativity'. The idea of an infinite interplay of particles, or impulses of energy, runs through our thinking both about the physical universe and about our position as individuals in that universe. A strong suggestion of the same indeterminacy arises from the technical study undertaken in this book. It has traced a transition from harmony based on

---

*Since these words were written, in 1952, Stravinsky has duly obliged, and used serial technique in some recent works.

chord-progression within a defined tonality, to the organization of texture on a basis of movement and interplay of strands and patterns, empirical combinations of sounds, and melodic lines set in endless variety of inter-relation. The same quest for new relationships characterizes the aesthetic as well as the technical approach in the art of the twentieth century. The inevitability of movement seems to be implied, not movement onwards to another stage, but movement as the essence of existence.

# GENERAL INDEX

# INDEX OF MUSICAL EXAMPLES